An Introduction to the Psalms

Other titles in the T&T Clark Approaches to Biblical Studies series include:

An Introduction to the Psalms

by

ALASTAIR G. HUNTER

t&t clark

Published by T & T Clark
A Continuum imprint
The Tower Building, 11 York Road, London SE1 7NX
80 Maiden Lane, Suite 704, New York, NY 10038

www.tandtclark.com

First published 2008

British Library Cataloguing-in-Publication Data
A catalogue record for this book is available from the British Library

ISBN-10: 0-567-03297-3 (hardback)
ISBN-13: 978-0-567-03297-3 (hardback)
ISBN-10: 0-567-03028-8 (paperback)
ISBN-13: 978-0-567-03028-3 (paperback)

Typeset by Free Range Book Design & Production Limited
Printed on acid-free paper in Great Britain by MPG Books Ltd,
Bodmin, Cornwall

Contents

Preface

In some ways a book like this is harder to write than a traditional monograph or paper. Reviewing the relevant literature without missing any significant work, and covering the range of topics which populate the field of study, are but two of the insistent demands of the genre. Add to these the requirement both to communicate sympathetically with potential readers who may well not have much of a grounding in the subject and to retain an appropriate level of scholarly discipline, and the challenges are clear. Maybe it would be better not to venture into these dangerous waters; yet there is an obvious need, recognizable by the fact that this book belongs to a series of similar introductions, to try to bridge the ever-increasing gap between professional scholarship and foundational studies.

At the same time, this writer – like all writers – is an individual with his own emphases and biases, his own pet theories and firm dislikes. My own idiosyncratic views will, I hope, have come across clearly; but I will have failed if they appear to predominate, or to forestall disagreement or different preferences on the part of the reader. Obviously there are many topics which have to be covered in a responsible guide to the discipline, so that freedom of movement is inevitably restricted. In my ordering of the material, and in the choice of chapter headings, I have sought some limited freedom (for instance, in dealing with groups of psalms before examining historical-critical issues); but it is my hope that no important area has been irresponsibly neglected. In any case, those otherwise disappointed will find in the extensive bibliography more than enough to keep them busy!

I have chosen quite deliberately to range across time in my treatment of secondary material. It is surprising (though it should not be) how often ideas we think to be 'modern' can be found in the work of scholars a couple of generations or more in the past. There is a fashion in scholarship as in most things: in Psalms study it is most notable in the swing between pre- and post-exilic theories of composition, and in the recurrent (roughly every seventy years!) proposal that some of the Psalms were specifically designed for the Maccabean regime. Here I ought to pay tribute to one 'lost' scholar – Cuthbert Keet. He was not a major figure in the field, and little turns up even on the internet relating to him. But he produced two useful books, one at the beginning of his career (in 1928, based on his Ph.D. thesis) and one towards the end, in 1969. Most of his professional life was spent as a priest in the Church of England, latterly in Cambridge. In bringing his name to the fore in this preface I offer a tribute both to this minor, individual, scholarly voice, and to the wealth of dedicated work that has been done by a myriad other teachers, researchers and lovers of the Psalms, for what they have given (anonymously) to us, who will in our turn soon be forgotten but for the accident of homages such as this.

As regards the living, I want to dedicate this volume to my daughter Jennifer, who has been a friend to me for longer than she would care to admit, and who might even be persuaded to read the work thus dedicated to her! I would like also to thank Steve Moyise, who has waited a long time (even allowing for the usual academic defiance of deadlines) for this volume, and to the publisher whose emails have kept me regularly (but not too persistently) aware of my commitments to them. And finally, to many students through the years of my teaching who are typical of the readers for whom this book is designed, I offer this introduction in the hope that they will recognize its origins in things they vaguely remember from seminars long past.

Alastair G. Hunter
8 May 2007

Note

Biblical references are to the NRSV, unless otherwise stated; verse numbering refers to the English convention, which means that many Psalms references will be out by a verse, or sometimes two, in respect of the Hebrew numbering.

Acknowledgements

The substance of Chapter 4 was first published as the article 'Psalms', in Andrew W. Hass, David Jasper and Elisabeth Jay (eds), *The Oxford Handbook of English Literature and Theology* (Oxford: Oxford University Press, 2007), pp. 243–58. The publisher's permission to use this material is gratefully acknowledged.

Chapter 1

Getting Started

1. Why study the Psalms?

It is a serious question. For many people of both Jewish and Christian backgrounds the book of Psalms is not the most obvious text to subject to the kind of scholarly attention that has delivered so many fascinating and contentious results over the two centuries of modern biblical criticism. They sing them or chant them or take comfort from them, and their familiar yet haunting phrases loom large in many people's personal life without benefit of source, form, or redaction criticism, textual study, or modern and postmodern reinterpretation. We call them 'the Psalms of David', using a romantic and a-historical shorthand in which a young shepherd forever clutches his lyre and strums the latest melody while fending off wild animals, Philistines and bad King Saul. Somewhere in the background is the tragic figure of Jonathan, a kind of John the Baptist to David's Christ; in darker tones there is Bathsheba – dynastic mother of Solomon, femme fatale, and possessor of a redundant husband, Uriah the Hittite. Bathsheba is forever the object, while bathing, of David's lustful gaze, while striding purposefully into the king's court is Nathan, the doomful prophet with a nice line in parables about pet lambs (see 2 Sam. 12.1-15).

In ancient times, too, it was normal to attach the Psalms to episodes in David's life, as if the poet-king had a pen beside him with which to jot down another apposite composition, even at the most extreme points of his life. Of these titles, some are quite simple ('A psalm of David') while others present the supposed occasion in some detail. Psalm 18, for example, informs us that it is 'A psalm of David the servant of the Lord, who addressed the words of this song to the Lord on the day when the Lord delivered him from the hand of all his enemies, and from the hand of Saul.' Psalm 51 is famous for its association with the Bathsheba situation: 'A psalm of David when

the prophet Nathan came to him, after he had gone in to Bathsheba.'
Even more curious is a title like that of Psalm 60, which goes into
considerable – and implausible – detail about an obscure conflict:
'A Miktam of David; for instruction; when he struggled with Aram-
naharaim and with Aram-zobah, and when Joab on his return killed
twelve thousand Edomites in the Valley of Salt.'

The validity of these connections is unclear, and the sensible
conclusion has to be that such accounts are a later effort to give
historical context to a genre which is essentially timeless. To be sure,
some of the words of Psalm 51 are fitting for the supposed situation;
thus verse 10:

> Create in me a clean heart, O God,
>   and put a new and right spirit within me.

But at the same time we find at the end (v. 18) an allusion which surely
has nothing to do with David's era:

> Do good to Zion in your good pleasure;
>   rebuild the walls of Jerusalem.

Such prayers are typically associated with the dreams of the exilic and
the post-exilic community, and cannot be linked with anything in
David's life. Yet the conceit that drives this mechanism remains very
strong, and still engenders a certain kind of pious commentary.

Personal experience is another deeply felt motivation for both the
use and the appreciation of psalms. The magnificent refrain of Psalm
8 ('O Lord, our Sovereign, how majestic is your name in all the earth')
together with its powerful and challenging theology:

> What are human beings that you are mindful of them,
>   mortals that you care for them?
> Yet you have made them a little lower than God,
>   and crowned them with glory and honour   (8.4-5)

contrives to be both inspiring and daunting, and gives a glimpse of
the kind of positive and affirmative theology which is so often lacking
in the more self-flagellatory forms of western Christianity. Of course,
this is only one side of the spiritual coin, for in a Psalm like 51 we
encounter an individual in the depths, profoundly aware of their own
failings, and desperate for healing, while the majestic words of the *De
Profundis* (Psalm 130), 'Out of the depths I cry to you, O Lord. Lord,
hear my voice' have repeatedly been set to music. Between these two

emotions, perhaps, is that of consolation and calm reflection, most familiarly expressed in Psalm 23 ('The Lord is my shepherd') but also notable in Psalms 27; 84 ('How lovely is your dwelling place, O Lord of hosts'; 'Even the sparrow finds a home ... at your altars, O Lord of hosts'; 'A day in your courts is better than a thousand elsewhere'); 121; 125; and 131. Another set of Psalms – the so-called Penitential Psalms – found a formal place in the Church's liturgies: they are 6; 32; 38; 51; 102; 130; and 143; it is not surprising to find Psalms 51 and 130 included here.

Another kind of experience is perhaps summed up in the language of battle and defeat, of God as triumphant overlord and the king as Messiah. Such psalms hardly connect with personal experience in the modern world, but they have been influential in the theological interpretation of the book of Psalms both in Judaism and in Christianity. The Dead Sea Scrolls provide evidence of an advanced messianic ideology in their reading of David in the Psalms – a topic we shall return to in Chapter 2 – and certain psalms have provided key texts for Christian claims about Christ. Two of the most significant are Psalms 2 and 110, cited respectively in the Gospel accounts of the baptism of Jesus and in the portrait of Jesus as messianic high priest in Hebrews 7. But it should not be concluded that this is a minor note in the Psalter as a whole: whatever they understood by the messiah, it is clear that Jewish communities of the intertestamental period saw that belief as a perfectly legitimate way to make sense of David's legacy, though they undoubtedly interpreted it in different ways; a useful survey of this topic is to be found in *Judaisms and Their Messiahs at the Turn of the Christian Era* (Neusner *et al.* 1987). Indeed, a composition like Psalm 132 so strongly demands such a reading that it is something of a wonder that the New Testament writers did not take it up. The last lines of this psalm (vv. 16-18) are imbued with the language of the ideal anointed 'David':

> Its priests I will clothe with salvation,
>> and its faithful will shout for joy.
> There I will cause a horn to sprout up for David;
>> I have prepared a lamp for my anointed one.
> His enemies I will clothe with disgrace,
>> but on him, his crown will gleam.

But defeat is also savoured: most memorably in the tragic poignancy and terrible vengeance of Psalm 137, in which the haunting opening words, 'By the waters of Babylon – there we sat down, and there we wept', stand in stark contrast with its disturbing final lines:

Happy shall they be who take your little ones
    and dash them against the rock!

Lesser known, but of profound sensitivity, is Psalm 55. This is one which is attributed to David, and it describes in memorable words the experience of being abandoned by those you thought were friends at the very time when they were most needed, when enemies surround the city. Thus vv. 12-14:

It is not enemies who taunt me –
    I could bear that;
it is not adversaries who deal insolently with me –
    I could hide from them.
But it is you, my equal,
    my companion, my familiar friend,
with whom I kept pleasant company;
    we walked in the house of God with the throng.

Not surprisingly a number of psalms take us into the realm of liturgy. Some were almost certainly liturgies in their original context, others have been adopted into Jewish or Christian worship, and many more have the feel of liturgical use even if we cannot directly demonstrate this function. A good example of the last kind is Psalm 24, whose last lines (vv. 7-10) have found a place in the eucharistic or communion liturgy of many Christian churches. I quote here the version found in the Scottish metrical Psalter, on the left, with the NRSV version set alongside for comparison. (Metrical psalms emerged as a striking contribution of the Reformation to liturgies in English. While these were often crude, at times they reached sublime poetic heights; and they certainly shaped popular access to the Psalms for most of the seventeenth to twentieth centuries. I will describe this phenomenon in more detail in Chapter 4):

Ye gates, lift up your heads on high:
    ye doors that last for aye,
Be lifted up, that so the King
    of glory enter may.
But who of glory is the king?
    The mighty Lord is this;
Ev'n that same Lord that great in might
    and strong in battle is.
	Lift up your heads, O gates!
	    and be lifted up, O ancient doors!
	    that the King of glory may come
	        in.
	Who is the King of glory?
	    The Lord, strong and mighty,
	    the Lord, mighty in battle.

Ye gates, lift up your heads; ye doors,	Lift up your heads, O gates!
doors that do last for aye,	and be lifted up, O ancient doors!
Be lifted up, that so the King	that the King of glory may come
of glory enter may.	in.
But who is he that is the King	Who is this King of glory?
of glory? Who is this?	The Lord of hosts,
The Lord of hosts, and none but he,	he is the King of glory.
the King of glory is.	

We know, from their being cited in 1 Chron. 16.8-36 and 2 Chron. 6.41-42, that Pss. 96.1-13; 105.1-15; and 132.8-10 almost certainly had a recognized role in the services of the temple. The first two are cited at the point where David places the ark in the sacred tent which preceded the temple, and where he also appoints named Levites to take charge of the appropriate worship. The 'ark' is sometimes known as 'the ark of God' and sometimes as 'the ark of the covenant'. It was a religious object which signified the might of Yahweh, and may have contained sacred objects. Some scholars think that it may have formed part of an empty throne which was significantly left bare of any iconic representation of the deity. The citation of Psalm 132 (itself overtly concerned with the ark) is in the context of the dedication of the temple in Solomon's reign. Further, the fact that Psalm 18 is quoted in its entirety in 2 Sam. 22 on David's lips as a triumph song is persuasive evidence that this composition also had a place in the regular liturgy, though it is now impossible to say precisely what that was.

One particular group of poems, Psalms 113–18, is known in Jewish tradition as 'the Hallel' and is linked in the Mishnah with different festivals, in particular Passover and Sukkot (or 'Booths': the autumn harvest festival, known in older English traditions as 'Tabernacles') 'Hallel' means 'praise', and is one element of the compound expression 'hallelujah' which means 'praise Yawheh'. It is easy to see why a group of psalms with a motif of that kind would find a place in worship; other psalms continue to be used in the synagogue liturgy, and I shall say more about this in Chapter 5. Finally, I have referred to psalms which are cited in other parts of the Old Testament in contexts which might suggest a liturgical purpose. There is another group of compositions which, while similar in form to those in the Psalter itself, are different in content. A good example is to be found in Exod. 15.1-17, where Moses and the Israelites sing a song of praise following their successful crossing of the Sea. It is possible, given that the story of the exodus from Egypt is closely bound up with Passover, that this provides an indication of the kind of psalm which might have been used in Passover liturgies in ancient times. Another instance in which a psalm-like composition is embedded in a prose narrative is to be found in the form of Hannah's prayer in 1 Sam. 2.1-10, which is in essence a psalm of thanksgiving. That she utters this song in the sanctuary of Shiloh when she dedicates Samuel to God's service might suggest two liturgical contexts: the dedication of the first-born son, and the celebration in more general terms of answered prayer.

One particular dimension of the Psalms merits special mention because of the problems it poses for many modern readers. Time and again the writers give expression in a most offensive manner to emotions of hatred, revenge and malice. They are unequivocal in the language they use regarding those who are held to be their enemies, wishing upon them all manner of plague, misfortune, punishment and imaginative death. The most notorious is undoubtedly the blessing in Ps. 137.9 concerning the Babylonians, 'Happy shall they be who take your little ones and dash them against the rock!'; but for sheer imaginative nastiness Ps. 58.6-8 is hard to beat:

> O God, break the teeth in their mouths;
>> tear out the fangs of the young lions, O Lord!
> Let them vanish like water that runs away;
>> like grass let them be trodden down and wither.
> Let them be like the snail that dissolves into slime;
>> like the untimely birth that never sees the sun.

Generally speaking there is a regular prayer that first identifies the wrongs suffered by the righteous (i.e. the psalmist and his or her people), then pleads with God for help, and concludes with a description of the punishment which God is expected to mete out. Psalm 11 affords a brief example which nicely illustrates this pattern. In the first three verses we read of an assault by the wicked, who are portrayed as skilful archers able to find their target in the dark:

> In the Lord I take refuge; how can you say to me,
>> 'Flee like a bird to the mountains;
> for look the wicked bend the bow,
>> they have fitted their arrow to the string,
>> to shoot in the dark at the upright in heart.'
> If the foundations are destroyed,
>> what can the righteous do?

The appeal to God takes the form of a reminder (vv. 4-5) that 'the Lord is in his holy temple' and that he will test and judge the wicked and the righteous:

> The Lord is in his holy temple;
> > the Lord's throne is in heaven.
> > His eyes behold, his gaze examines humankind.
> The Lord tests the righteous and the wicked,
> > and his soul hates the lover of violence.

The punishment which ensues (v. 6) is swift and dramatic:

> On the wicked he will rain coals of fire and sulphur;
> > a scorching wind shall be the portion of their cup.

Finally the righteous receive a promise that they shall see God's face (v. 7) because the Lord loves righteous deeds:

> For the Lord is righteous;
> he loves righteous deeds;
> > the upright shall behold his face.

The reference to the cup is significant in the light of another, very familiar psalm. We do not usually associate Psalm 23 with this theme of revenge, but there is a subtle use of it in verse 5:

> You prepare a table before me
> > in the presence of my enemies;
> you anoint my head with oil;
> > my cup overflows.

Notice that the cup now signifies blessing, and the blessing is enhanced by the fact that the psalmist's enemies have to look on enviously as God showers favours on the chosen. A more subtle revenge, perhaps, but still smacking a little of triumphalism. The cup of blessing and salvation is also mentioned, incidentally, in Ps. 116.13, where it may have a direct relevance to the Passover ritual.

We might try to dispose of this aspect of the Psalms, perhaps, by regarding it as a primitive response which is unworthy of more advanced and civilized societies. Unfortunately there is little evidence to suggest that – in matters of revenge and our instinctive response to perceived grievances – we are emotionally much different from the Israelites. A more specific form of this explanation is to suggest that this was a pre-Christian response which had not yet benefited from the message of love brought to the world by Jesus. But this too represents sloppy thinking. It is the God of Jesus who slays Ananias and Sapphira

(Acts 5.1-11) for no worse a crime than falsifying their offerings. It is the God of the New Testament who prepares a vast, eternal, and painful hell for those who fail to become Christian. And it is the God of the Old Testament of whom we read, several times in different places, 'you are a gracious God and merciful, slow to anger and abounding in steadfast love, and ready to relent from punishing'. This example is from Jon. 4.2, in the context of the prophet Jonah's bitter resentment that God had indeed exercised such mercy by forgiving (on very little evidence) the entire corrupt and violent city of Nineveh. Undoubtedly this is an aspect not just of the Psalms, but of scripture more generally, which is troublesome to a modern conscience; the solution is not easy to find, unless of course we are ready to admit that justice (whether human or divine) is brutal and unsophisticated, and is strictly punitive without any reformative intent. One possible way out, with respect at least to the Psalms, was suggested, among others, by C.S. Lewis (1958: 20–33): it is better to work out our feelings of revenge and hatred towards our enemies in prayer than to indulge them in actual deeds of violence. The psalmists, on this reading, are engaging in a cathartic – and honest – attempt to face the dark side of their desires, and by speaking of them openly, enabling a process of exorcism of these troubling demons. The reader must reach his or her own conclusion as to the viability of this explanation.

2. Techniques and critical methods

In the second part of this introductory overview I want to make reference to the various ways in which the scholarly community has tried to explain the Psalms over the century or so since the pioneering work of Hermann Gunkel. In effect, having asked why, as a general reader, one might want to engage with the Psalms, I now turn to a consideration of the motivations of those whose starting point is in the academic world. Questions of a historical kind have dominated research for many years. Who wrote the Psalms? When were they composed, or edited, or collected? What purpose did they serve when they were first produced, and can we identify changes in their use through time? How reliable is our Hebrew text? The Psalms appear to be in the form of poetry – and this is confirmed by the existence of manuscripts from the Dead Sea Scrolls which set them out according to the delineation we are familiar with. If this is so, what difference does that make to how we interpret them? To what extent do the 'rules' of parallelism matter, or such rarefied concerns as metre and rhythm – indefinable because we can no longer interrogate native speakers, and the accents and vowels we now have were added many centuries later. Most of these concerns are covered in detail in standard critical introductions to the Psalms, such as Gillingham (1994) and Seybold (1990), and it would be inappropriate to duplicate that work here. But some general observations are in order.

Of all the classic approaches to the study of the Psalms, that of Gunkel has dominated, to the extent that almost every commentary automatically includes a form-critical description with its remarks on each individual psalm. Some discussions, indeed, focus almost exclusively on that one issue, as if the task of classification were the only one that mattered, and the decision as to a psalm's form the sole key to its meaning. Of course Gunkel himself intended no such thing, and he would, I believe, have been horrified to think that what was a means to an end had become an end in itself. The fundamental principle is plausible: if we can identify the literary features of a given psalm as characteristic of a certain form, it might be possible then to work back to the 'original' purpose for which the psalm was composed or the context in which it was used – the *Sitz-im-Leben*. I shall discuss Gunkel's contribution in more detail in Chapter 3; in the meantime we may note some examples which appear to be susceptible to this treatment in a quite straightforward way. Psalm 2 is – surely? – a coronation liturgy, while Psalm 15 exemplifies the kind of formal 'interrogation' that pilgrims could expect as they approached the gates of the temple. Psalms of praise, like the group which brings the Psalter to a rousing conclusion (145–150), can readily be understood as a resource for those occasions when it was appropriate to sing hymns of joyful celebration. The festivals of Sukkot and Shevuot (literally, 'weeks'; the early summer festival which later become known as Pentecost – literally 'fifty days', because it took place seven weeks after Passover; the equivalent in the Christian cycle of festivals is Whitsun) spring to mind as likely candidates; but they might just as well have figured in whatever Sabbath services were observed in ancient Israel. The fact, already noted, that the Hallel (Psalms 113–18) is, according to the Mishnah, used in more than one festival lends credence to this idea of multiple functions for key psalms.

More problematic are psalms in which an individual seems to bewail his (or her?) personal circumstances. While such laments are perfectly understandable as a form of prayer with which people of many religions would be familiar, it is not so easy to see how they found their way into a public collection. Were some of them written by persons, now unknown, who were of sufficient standing (and literacy!) in their day for their private musings to have been saved for posterity? The most famous of all such individuals is, of course,

David; but, as we have already seen, this attribution is by no means secure. There is, for example, no evidence that David was literate! The explanation most commonly resorted to by followers of Gunkel's approach is that such psalms are not really individual; rather they are expressions of the community's concerns voiced *as if* each worshipper were individually praying. We might readily imagine that psalms of this kind could have been used either as special prayers in time of difficulty (Assyrians or Babylonians at the gate, for example), or at those points in the feast of unleavened bread and the Passover when the solemn events of the oppression in Egypt were recalled.

Finding a plausible *occasion* for a psalm could then form the starting point of a rereading of it in which the setting derived from its form was used to explain what the writer was striving to communicate. This is not a purely circular exercise, for if the form is defined by objective criteria (such as the presence of specific words or phrases, or a particular style), then the idiosyncratic detail remains to be explained. Compare, for example, Psalms 135 and 148. Both are marked as items of praise, beginning and ending with the formula 'Praise the Lord'. But the specific content is markedly different, for the former uses the history of God's violence against enemy nations as the occasion of the psalmist's glee, while the latter celebrates the God of creation whose praise is sung by both inanimate bodies, like the sun, the moon and the stars; and living creatures, whether wild, domesticated or human. Vastly different psalms, then, though capable of being classified under a single heading, and obviously demanding quite different hermeneutical strategies.

This is all very well; but a further complication should be noted. There are signs that at some point *within* the development of the book of Psalms, and before it was canonically completed, it changed in character – whether gradually or suddenly we do not know – from being a liturgical handbook to functioning as a collection of sources for pious or theological reflection. There are at least two kinds of evidence for this. First, among the Dead Sea Scrolls are found collections of psalms which focus very specifically on the role of David as king/messiah, and whose raison d'être therefore is to be found within the community's emphasis on the role of the righteous teacher and on messianic expectations. But, from another angle entirely, the special character of Psalms 1 and 2 has frequently been remarked upon. They are *not* labelled as 'of David', they seem to form a preface to the collection as a whole, and they appear to direct the individual reader to a certain reflective way of reading these works. When taken together with the long alphabetical Psalm 119 and its excessive celebration of Torah, there is a case to be made that we have here a form of the book of Psalms which emerged at some stage – prior to final canonization – as a book for private or learned study. Claus Westermann's *Praise and Lament in the Psalms* (1981: 252–3) seems to be the primary source of this suggestion. The German original was published in 1965, and B.S. Childs refers to it in his influential *Introduction to the Old Testament as Scripture* (1979: 513). These are plausible proposals, and dates for their development can be suggested. For the moment all I want to do is to indicate that, at the very least, Psalms 1 and 2 may be pastiches or imitations of traditional forms intended to alert the reader to significant themes. If so, then the quest for a *Sitz-im-Leben* takes on a quite different character, for there would then not necessarily be any direct cultural context in (say) a coronation ritual. Rather we would be looking for models of such ceremonies contemporary with the possible date of composition. Merely setting out this possibility demonstrates just how problematic Gunkel's approach can be. It by no means invalidates it, but certainly warns us against overly simplistic analyses. An interesting parallel case is that of Genesis 14, which appears to be an ancient historical chronicle – and has been so interpreted by many commentators. But the presence of very serious anachronisms in the chapter, and its awkward positioning within the broader Abrahamic materials, have suggested to others that this is more like romantic historical fiction than a genuine record of ancient events.

Gunkel's work in turn informed a second major line of attack, most significantly represented by the work of Sigmund Mowinckel and A.R. Johnson. This consisted of a sustained effort to provide an overall festival context for the book of Psalms which would take account not only of the setting of individual compositions, but of groups of psalms. In part this was a response to the evident fact that the book as it stands cannot be clearly related to any of the principal biblical festivals. In Mowinckel's case, the work of Gunkel in identifying types such as the lament of the individual and so on was influential in his identification of aspects of proposed 'restored' festivals. Johnson took a more esoteric approach in which he identified concealed elements in a number of psalms which pointed to a forgotten enthronement festival which bore many similarities to the Babylonian festival of Marduk. The temptation to rediscover liturgical sequences or events has remained strong, and reappears in such work as that of Goulder (1982) on the psalms attributed to Korah, and my own *Psalms* in which I postulate a Maccabean festival represented by the Psalms of Ascents (Hunter 1999: 181–82, 242–48). At some level all of these must be purely speculative, in the absence of corroborative evidence; but their inherent plausibility – quite apart from the likelihood of any one of them being correct – is persuasive. This is further confirmed by efforts to demonstrate the use of psalms in a kind of liturgical afterlife: thus Trudinger's study of the Tamid Psalms (2004), which are in the Mishnah associated with a particular daily service, and the application of the Hallel Psalms to several Jewish festivals in Mishnah which we have already noted. We may add to this the supposition often made that they had some kind of liturgical function in the Christian Last Supper, where Jesus and the disciples are recorded as singing a hymn (Mt. 26.30).

Despite the predominance of form-critical approaches, other dimensions of Psalms study began to receive significant attention in the last quarter of the twentieth century. A renewed interest in parallelism and in the poetry of the Psalms emerged in the work of scholars such as Kugel (1981), Watson (1984) and Berlin (1985). While not the only academics to investigate this field, each has contributed a classic study on the poetry of the Psalms which together have defined and to some extent dominated this development. As with form criticism, it is not possible in a brief overview to represent their work in any detail. A more extended treatment of the poetry of the Psalms will be found, for example, in Chapter 4 of my own reader (Hunter 1999: 46–61).

The significance of parallelism was recognized early in the traditions of interpretation practised by the Rabbis from the eleventh century onwards. Classical rabbinic exegesis tended to treat repetitions as having a predominantly semantic role in adding additional halakhic aspects beyond those which can be deduced from the simple statement. Thus the repetition of a word, phrase or story, for example, was seen not primarily as a rhetorical device, but as a matter of further legal significance. Among the rabbinic scholars of eleventh- and twelfth-century northern France, however, a more literary approach can be discerned in which the *poetic* function of parallelism was recognized (Harris 2004). Rashi, Rashbam, Rabbi Eliezer of Beaugency, and Rabbi Joseph Bekhor Shor were aware of its rhetorical force, and also deployed it – as many modern exegetes have – to elucidate puzzling texts. Thus a rare word or an obscure phrase can be interpreted if it is in obvious parallel with a familiar word or phrase. Rashbam, in his commentary on Deut. 32.23, interprets the more obscure verb in the second half of the verse on the assumption that its meaning is to be discerned on the basis of a more common one in the first half. I have set out Rashbam's reading in parallel with that of the NRSV to illustrate this point (Harris 2004: 57–8):

Rashbam	NRSV
I will use up upon them evils	I will heap disasters upon them,
I will finish [my arrows against them]	spend my arrows against them.

It is a matter of familiar record that the introduction of the study of parallelism as a major dimension of poetic analysis of the Psalms is due to Robert Lowth's groundbreaking work in the eighteenth century (Lowth 1787 [1847]); it is important to recognize, nevertheless, that he in turn was at least indirectly indebted to earlier rabbinic scholarship.

Parallelism as a phenomenon is not, of course, unique either to Hebrew or to cognate Semitic languages, nor is it confined to poetry. The urge to clarify by repetition, to express oneself through synonym, contrast or even contradiction, is arguably a universal feature of language. Indeed, the preceding sentence is an example of just that! Nevertheless it is undeniable that it reached a particularly developed form in Hebrew poetry, though its antecedents in older Canaanite language are clear. Ugaritic poetry, which is known to us through the texts found at Ras Shamra in the 1920s, bears many similarities to Hebrew poetry, though the city in which it was spoken was destroyed and abandoned by around 1200 BCE. Whatever the wider significance of these similarities, they at least serve to remind us of the long literary (oral and written) tradition to which Hebrew belonged, and of the wider cultural world beyond the hill country of Judah or the fertile valleys of Samaria and Galilee.

Parallelism is relatively easy to convey in translation, unlike other characteristic Hebrew poetic devices such as assonance, alliteration and word-play or paronomasia. Alternatives based on metre are effectively lost to us, since we no longer know how the language was spoken or stressed; and rhyme in the European sense is irrelevant. Such rhyme as exists is best seen as a form of assonance. Since Hebrew is a heavily inflected language, with many standard suffixes, end-rhyme is simply trivial, being far too easy to achieve and so having little effect and status as a Hebrew poetic form. The desirability of reporting parallelism in English translation is, in consequence, obvious. Difficulties arise because natural word order in Hebrew is different from that in English. Hebrew is a verb–subject–object (VSO) language, whereas English is typically subject–verb–object (SVO). Moreover, a Hebrew verb embeds its pronominal subject within the form, and can carry a pronominal object as a suffix. Thus a simple sentence like 'The king ordered him to go' is conveyed in Hebrew by something like 'He-ordered-him the-king to-go', where hyphenated forms indicate a single 'word' in Hebrew. But even in English, poetry has licence to disrupt 'normal' order; thus more could be achieved in this respect than is allowed by traditional biblical translations. Ps. 121.3-6 provides a good example. The literal Hebrew is on the left, NRSV is on the right:

v. 3 He shall not let slip your feet
    he will not slumber,
    <u>who keeps you.</u>
	He will not let your foot be moved;
	    <u>he who keeps</u> you will not
	    slumber.

v. 4 Behold, he will not slumber,
    nor will he sleep,
    <u>who keeps Israel.</u>
	<u>He who keeps Israel</u> will
	    neither slumber
	    nor sleep.

v. 5 It is Yahweh who keeps you
    Yahweh is your shade at your
    right hand.
	The Lord is your keeper,
	    the Lord is your shade at your
	    right hand.

v. 6 <u>By day</u> the sun shall not strike you,
    nor the moon at night.
	The sun shall not strike <u>you by day</u>,
	    nor the moon by night

The poetic force of the Hebrew version is greater, in my estimation, in three respects. First, its use in verse 5 of a verbal (participial) form 'who keeps' is preferable to the more prosaic 'your keeper'. Since the NRSV uses the verbal form elsewhere, this seems a curious departure. Second, the delay of the subject 'who keeps you' and 'who keeps Israel' to the end of verses 3 and 4 ensures a creative tension which is lacking in the English. And third, the structure of v.6 is actually chiastic: that is, it has the form A–B–C–B*–A* which is turned into a simple parallel form B–C–A // B*–[C]–A* in the English. (By placing the second C in square brackets we indicate that the same verb serves double duty in the verse, though it is not actually repeated). While there may not be much to choose between them aesthetically, it seems to me proper to preserve the Hebrew order where possible: my claim is that in this case it is perfectly possible.

The principal features and functions of parallelism may be summed up as follows:

a. Forms

1. Simple synonymous repetition. Example (Ps. 19.1-2):

The heavens are telling	the glory of God;
and the firmament proclaims	his handiwork.
Day to day	pours forth speech,
and night to night	declares knowledge.

2. 'Crossed' or chiastic repetition. Example (Ps. 58.7):

Let them vanish	like water that runs away;
like grass	let them be trodden down and wither.

3. Antithetic or contrasting repetition, which can of course be either synonymous or chiastic.
   Example (1 Sam. 2.7: synonymous):

   | The Lord makes poor | and makes rich |
   | he brings low | he also exalts. |

   Example (Ps. 1.6: chiastic):

   | for the Lord watches over | the way of the righteous |
   | but the way of the wicked | will perish. |

4. Climactic parallelism, where there is a build-up to a concluding dramatic statement. Example (Ps. 29.1-2):

Ascribe to the Lord,	O heavenly beings,
ascribe to the Lord	glory and strength.
Ascribe to the Lord	the glory of his name;
worship the Lord in	
holy splendour.	

5. 'Step' or 'staircase' parallelism, where the end of one line is repeated at the beginning of the next. Example (Ps. 94.1):

   | O Lord, | you God of vengeance, |
   | you God of vengeance | shine forth! |

While many of the instances of parallelism can be subsumed under one or other of these headings – and often under several of them together – it is wise to have regard to Kugel's definition: 'Biblical parallelism is of one sort, "A, and what's more, B", or a hundred sorts; but it is not three' (Kugel 1981: 58; his reference to three is to synonymous, antithetic and chiastic parallelism), which can serve as a warning against being overly prescriptive, and as a reminder of something we noted at the beginning of this discussion: that *all* language makes use, to a greater or lesser extent, of parallels. What characterizes poetry is the *density* of its use of this phenomenon.

b. Functions

1. It is important to recognize at the outset that parallelism has an artistic or aesthetic function. All poets are creative linguistic artists, and parallelism is part of the sheer pleasure of poetry.
2. It also has a rhetorical function – the desire to reinforce an argument or to make a point more dramatically.
3. Parallelism can also serve to clarify: to give a particular instance following a general statement, to elucidate a consciously rare or

anachronistic form, or to add additional meaning – particularly in a surprising way, when the reader might have thought a conclusion had been reached.

4. It also has a structural purpose. The overall pattern of a poem is made up of the small structures of its individual verses and lines, within which parallelism operates to greatest effect. But it can also appear on the wider canvas of the whole composition. The simplest example of this is the use of refrains, which appear in several psalms.

In the rest of this book we will look at a range of topics in greater detail, and provide further published material which should enable the reader to find his or her way deeper into the study of what is, for all its difficulties, a most rewarding field of study.

Chapter 2

The Diversity of Collections of Psalms

M ost students of the Psalms will encounter them either through a commentary, which will traditionally begin with Psalm 1 and follow the numerical order of the book until the relief that is Psalm 150, or by means of an introduction. Commentaries as a genre are not designed to be read through from beginning to end, and this is even more so of commentaries on the Psalms. And introductions have a duty to cover the ground, to let the reader know where the discipline is at by providing an overview of approaches and generally agreed results. The present modest volume seeks to distance itself from both of these approaches, not because either is to be faulted, but in the interests of a fresh(er) starting point for those who have not yet been fully inducted into the mysteries of the discipline. In this regard it should be considered as a companion (perhaps *prequel* is the best description) to my *Psalms* (Hunter 1999), which attempted to forge a new(er) way to do commentary on the Psalms. I shall provide an overview of commentaries and introductions in Chapter 7.

It is for this reason that, rather than opening with an account of forms and genres, as John Day does in his Sheffield introduction (Day 1990), I have chosen to address at the outset a question which is intuitively obvious but which until relatively recently has been somewhat marginalized. I refer to the task of taking into account the headings which define smaller groups of psalms, as distinct from those which purport to provide a historical context. It is of interest to note that the two other general introductions which are currently available – Klaus Seybold (1990), and S.E. Gillingham (1994) – also delay treatment of the form-critical classification of the Psalms, preferring to begin with matters of poetic structure and historical concern. Neither, however, prioritizes the grouping of psalms. As Gunkel noted long ago (1933 [1998]: 8), the historical headings are quite simply spurious as witnesses to any genuine antiquity: 'It seems at first that [in the psalm superscriptions] we possess a solid foundation. But that is only how it appears, because this tradition is attested much too late and certainly includes secondary elements.' But the fact of the grouping together of psalms bearing the name 'Korah', for example, which is also attested in the Chronicler's arrangements for the cult, might *prima facie* have some pertinence to our investigations. To this rather simple premise I shall add two others: the possibility that even where headings and titles do not provide groupings, there might be linguistic or thematic congruences which could assist in the business of interpretation; and the relevance of evidence of arrangement by 'editors' – whether we mean those within what emerged as the mainstream tradition (assuming that their traces can be identified), or those in alternative contexts evidenced by such phenomena as the Dead Sea Scrolls, the Septuagint, and the Syriac Psalms. The dominant Psalms tradition is that represented in Hebrew Bible editions since the sixteenth century. It is in turn based on the Hebrew text edited between the sixth and the ninth centuries by a scholarly succession known as the Masoretes. In honour of them this standard edition is known as the *Masoretic Text* (MT). Both the Dead Sea Scrolls (significantly) and the Septuagint (marginally) diverge from MT. What I hope will emerge from this approach is a clearer sense of a living, developing corpus of works whose relevance is continually renewed as the communities to whom they belong develop and change.

Many of the explanations which will be examined in this chapter are more than usually speculative – necessarily so, since both the people and the contexts to which smaller groups may have belonged are for the most part irretrievably lost. Nevertheless the quest for understanding at this level is itself enlightening, and casts sometimes surprising light on the relationship of the Psalms to the rest of scripture. The Psalter is usually divided into five books (I.1-41, II.42-72, III.73-89, IV.90-106, V.107-150), yet the only psalms directly cited in liturgical contexts in Chronicles come from Books IV and V – arguably the latest to have been collected or composed. The one psalm from earlier sections which is quoted *in extenso* is Psalm 18, used not as liturgy, but as a song of thanksgiving in 2 Samuel 22 towards the end of David's life, apparently summing up his military successes. Other compositions of a similar nature to psalms are used in association with Moses (Exod. 15.1-18; Deut. 32.1-43), Jonah (Jon. 2.2-9), Hannah (1 Sam. 2.1-10) and Deborah (Judges 5), all reflecting a historicized and individualistic application of this kind of material. Does this suggest that the writers of Exodus and Deuteronomy, Judges, Samuel and Jonah were already conscious of the earlier Psalms as a somewhat antiquarian mode of worship, suitable for inclusion in their representations of the history of past times and heroes of old? It is an interesting speculation, perhaps reinforced by the claim, noted in Chapter 1, that Psalms 1 and 2 together with 118 and 119 form a bracketing of an edition of the Psalter already perceived as a book for private study and messianic speculation. Psalms 1 and 119, in this hypothesis, emphasize particularly the need for contemplative study based on the primacy of the Torah, while 2 and 118 can be understood as psalms with a royal or messianic thrust.

1. The Psalms of Ascents

The earliest group of psalms to attract attention in its own right was the sequence from 120 to 134 which bear the unique title 'A song of ascents, *or* degrees'. We shall have occasion to refer to a number of studies of these psalms as we discuss their importance; a list of other works is provided at the end of this chapter. The Hebrew, *shir hamma'alot*, is of unclear meaning, and this unclarity has contributed to the range of interpretation of what they might be about. The Rabbis affirmed that they were sung on fifteen steps of the temple (*M. Middoth* ii.5; compare *M. Sukkah* v.4), thus providing a very literal interpretation of 'ascents' as 'steps'. This ceremony took place on the first day of Sukkot, a not-implausible festival with which to associate these psalms; however, this explanation is almost certainly fanciful, since there is no ancient testimony to it, and the rabbinic claim was made long after the temple had disappeared. In modern times the group attracted a book-length study by Keet (1969), whose thesis was that the Psalms of Ascents could be associated with the offering of the first-fruits (*bikkurim*) at the temple at Pentecost (*shavuot*). Two aspects of Keet's study remain valuable: the introductory section (pp. 1–17) in which he evaluates the range of interpretations offered from the time of the Mishnah to Mowinckel's association of them with his speculative New Year Enthronement Festival; and a section (pp. 112–34) in which he describes their use in Jewish life and liturgy.

Further studies by Loren Crow (1996) and, as part of a wider study, by myself (Hunter 1999) offered diverse interpretations. Crow's emphasis lay on the redactional nature of these psalms, but he also provided considerable detail describing the internal consistency of the group in linguistic terms, listing examples of the characteristic language and syntax which sets them apart as a distinctive group, quite apart from their titles. His conclusion was that they represent a rhetorical device, a propaganda collection specific to the Persian period and designed to encourage all Jews everywhere to see Jerusalem as the source of their prosperity and the focus of their religious identity. Thus he rejects both the notion that this group has been specifically composed, in favour of a more eclectic process, and the idea that they have a specific bearing on an actual liturgy. Using the same evidence and building upon it, I worked out a case in detail for the thesis that the Psalms of Ascents were composed as a coherent set of songs relating to a pilgrimage liturgy. In arguing this case I adopted the interpretation of 'ascents' which uses its derivation from the verb 'to go up on pilgrimage' which is clearly attested elsewhere in the Old Testament. Finally, I speculated that this specific group could have been developed or adapted to meet the particular needs of the Maccabean kings of the Hasmonaean dynasty, which ruled from about 140 to 67 BCE.

Taking a different approach entirely, Michael Goulder (1998) studied the Psalms of Ascents within the context of a complex liturgy surrounding the innovative policies of Nehemiah and the returning exiles who took control of the apparatus of the Jerusalem temple and the Judaean city state from about 450 BCE. The Psalms of Ascents, in this reading, form a Levitical response to Nehemiah's own words celebrating the return to Jerusalem and the restoration of its walls and temple. In adopting this approach Goulder echoes a traditional, though flawed reading of Ps. 126.1, 'When the Lord brought back those who returned to Zion' (NRSV footnote). Though he accepts the majority reading which prefers to interpret the undoubtedly difficult Hebrew of this verse as does the main NRSV text: 'When the Lord restored the fortunes of Zion', his emphasis nonetheless seems more in the spirit of that older reading. Incidentally, he is also unequivocal in his conviction that these psalms represent a compositional unity. He deploys much of the same evidence that is used by Crow and myself, though his conclusion in this regard is closer to mine.

One final comment is of importance in this brief overview: it is well known that the great Psalms scroll from the Dead Sea represents a rather different version of the Psalter, with the contents of Books IV and V in particular showing significant digression from the Masoretic Text (MT) 'norm'. However, within this diversity it is noteworthy that the Psalms of Ascents form a more or less constant grouping, suggesting that they were well known to those from Qumran whose interests were theological and messianic, and in consequence were preserved in their familiar order. This fits with the fact that 2 Chron. 6.40-42 seems to refer to Psalms 130 and 132 within the liturgical context of Solomon's prayer for wisdom. See also Goulder (1998: 28), where he points out that the Chronicler 'alters Solomon's Prayer of 1 Kgs 8 to bring it into line with Pss. 130 and 132'.

2. The Psalms of Korah and of Asaph

Leaving the relatively settled waters of the Psalms of Ascents, I turn next to two puzzling groups which have also received attention in recent decades: the Psalms of Korah and the Psalms of Asaph. Not least of the puzzles is that while these titles appear to refer to personal names, we really know little or nothing about the owners of these titles, or what their special significance was. The names are found in Chronicles, in connection with the organization of the service of the temple (presumably relating to some point in the later post-exilic period), though the name of Korah is also associated with a fatal revolt during the wilderness period, recorded in Num. 16.1-40. Asaph is recorded in 1 Chron. 16.5 (cf. 25.1-8) as the leader of the singers appointed by David to praise God when the ark was placed in the tent prepared for it when it was brought to Jerusalem (16.1-42). This is a clearly anachronistic passage which assumes the whole ritual of the temple in advance of Solomon's construction of the shrine. The sons of Asaph are mentioned again in the context of the cleansing of the temple under Hezekiah (2 Chron. 29.13), and reference is made in the same chapter (v. 30) to the Levites singing 'praises to the Lord with the words of David and of the seer Asaph', a formula which seems to suggest Asaph as a composer of liturgical materials alongside David. Finally, Asaph is one of the Levitical groups with responsibilities in Josiah's passover (2 Chron. 35.15). Korah is mentioned as one of the families of gatekeepers in 1 Chron. 26.1; the significance of this duty is not clear, though it would appear that it was lesser than that of the directors of music. There is a possible parallel in 2 Chron. 31.14 (the form of the name here is Kore), but on the whole the place of the Korahites is much less prominent, though they do appear in the context of Jehoshaphat's lament in 2 Chron. 20.19.

Within the Psalms these 'groups' suffer from being somewhat dispersed, lacking the straightforward coherence of the Ascents, and lacking also any obvious shared and distinctive language. The Korah Psalms are found in 42; 44–49; 84–85; and 87–88, and those of Asaph in 50 and 73–83. Clearly any case that is made in respect of these 'groups' has to take into account their fragmented nature. In essence, the Psalms of Korah are in two groups (42–49 and 84–88; it is possible to embrace the two odd untitled psalms as belonging by default). Those of Asaph constitute most of Book III, with one 'stray' at the end of the first Korah set. It may be that a thesis combining these two in some overarching context could be reached; this would in effect create a run from 42 to 50 and then from 73 to 88, separated by a group mostly entitled 'Of David', the exceptions being 71, which has no title, and 72, which is entitled 'Of Solomon' – a rare dedication, though it does occur in the Psalms of Ascents, at 127. Goulder's first three studies of groups of psalms dealt with these three sets: Korah (1982), the Prayers of David (51–72) (1990), and Asaph (1996) and Harry Nasuti contributed a separate study of the Psalms of Asaph in 1988. True to Goulder's long-established interest in liturgies integrated with historical recitals (see, for example, his early work on Matthew as a lectionary), he finds evidence, through his detailed examination of the language of the Psalms and geographical and historical clues within them, of processionals and festivals associated both with Dan and with Jerusalem.

Goulder's explanation for the double set of Korah psalms is rooted in a historical link with the Northern sanctuary of Dan, where the group is supposed to have originated in the context of an autumn festival of the ninth and eighth centuries. The existence of two separate Korah groups can be explained on the hypothesis that what was originally a joyful festival, represented by 84–85; 87–89, became less relevant with the decline in Israel's fortunes after the death of Jeroboam II, leading to a transformation in which a group of more downbeat compositions (42–49) takes the place of the original set, without their being expunged from the collection as a whole. Goulder argues for a pairing of the psalms in the later group with those in the earlier: his sequence runs: 42, 43, 84; 44, 85; 45, 46; 47, 48, 87; 49, 88. The last psalm in the sequence, 89, is not headed 'Of Korah'; but it does share the title 'Maskil' with Psalm 88. Goulder's claim is that it represents the reworking and expansion of an earlier Korahite composition in order to adapt the whole sequence to occupy a legitimate place in the liturgy of the Jerusalem establishment. Part of this process involved the addition of the sequence of Davidic Psalms (and one attributed to Solomon) which we have already noted in the 'gap' between 49 and 73. As with all of Goulder's reinterpretations, there is a considerable emphasis on what to contemporary readers might seem to be a rather uncritical view of history – in this case that of the two kingdoms as represented by the Deuteronomist. But he never fails to provide a close and expert reading of the text of each psalm, and is adept at discovering (if not conjuring) relevant links both within the group and to his proposed historical foundations.

Turning to the Psalms of Asaph, Nasuti's findings are more literary in form, though he does nevertheless link the psalms to liturgical contexts. Moreover, on the basis of certain similarities of language and theme, he extends his review to include a group of Asaph-like psalms (specifically 95; 96; 100; 105; and 106) which are quoted by the Chronicler in 1 Chronicles 16 in the context of Asaph. His analysis is heavily dependent on a tradition-historical approach which assumes the reality of a prior tradition-stream known as the Ephraimite, coined by Robert R. Wilson (1980). He makes a number of points about the characteristic features of this group: (a) Four communal laments constitute the core of the group (74; 79; 80; and 83); (b) This may indicate a communal ceremony of some kind; thus

> the presence of communal laments among the Asaphite psalms would seem to indicate for the *traditio* group behind the psalms a role in, or at least some connection with, the ceremonies of communal lamentation. ... One such narrative description may be found in 2 Chronicles 20. In this passage, a complete ceremony of national lamentation is described, including its situation and its consequences. (Nasuti 1988: 120; as a matter of fact, it is Korah, not Asaph, who appear in this passage)

(c) The Psalms of Asaph are uniformly concerned with military rather than natural disasters; and 74 and 79 have long been associated with the destruction of the temple; (d) Certain psalms within the group have been seen as belonging to specific ceremonies in ancient Israel. These observations, and the evident link (through the 'deutero-asaphite' psalms) with Chronicles, amount to a case for an Asaphite tradition in the communal lament ceremonies of second-temple Jerusalem.

As with Goulder's treatment, there are several assumptions which have to be granted and questions begged before Nasuti's results can be accepted, and whether the evidence adduced is strong enough to bear the weight of the conclusions drawn may be doubted. Given that the link with Chronicles is based on the somewhat dubious assumption that the psalms quoted by that book in liturgical contexts are 'honorary' Asaphite psalms, we must in the end remain sceptical about the liturgical contexts proposed, without necessarily rejecting Nasuti's more general observations.

The Psalms of Asaph constituted Goulder's third venture into the territory – he previously discussed the Psalms of David in Book II – and once again he sought an extensive historical correlation, this time with the Pentateuch. This may seem somewhat counter-intuitive given that most commentators have noted significant thematic and linguistic connections between Book III and the exilic materials found in Jeremiah and Lamentations. The link with the Pentateuch is retrospective, in that the setting of the psalms as they are now found suggests a lost temple and cultus. Nevertheless, he deploys his customary exegetical skills to construct a case, even if in the end it must be judged to be less than persuasive. Specifically, Goulder's thesis is that 'the Psalms of Asaph were composed in Northern Israel in response to the Assyrian threat, and were then taken and reused in a (slightly) edited form in Jerusalem to fit the conditions of the Babylonian destruction of the Temple in 587' (Goulder 1996: 36). And in a barnstorming conclusion, Goulder builds upon his work on Korah and Asaph to present a thesis that it was these very circles who were responsible for the Deuteronomistic edition of the Pentateuch which we now own. This is, if a failure, a magnificent one, and we can only applaud its daring while remarking (perhaps on a rather minor key) that it remains the case that the most coherent interpretation of the Psalms of Asaph is in relation to the traumatic destruction of the temple by the Babylonians, perhaps contextualized and theologically explained as a proper judgement upon the Judaeans for their falseness and failure to worship Yahweh as they should. The explanation of the 'stray' Asaphite Psalm 50 could be that a psalm which originally represented a lament for and judgement on the faithless kingdom of Israel (50.7) is appropriated by the application of a suitable title, and by the neutralizing of the reference to Israel with a clear sign that it is the God of Zion (Jerusalem) (v. 2) who is issuing judgement. The sequence of Davidic psalms which follows, ending with one attributed to Solomon, then forms a reprise of the experience of monarchy as a united kingdom against the backdrop of which the final loss of the remnant kingdom of Israel is all the more poignant.

3. Books III and IV

Robert Cole (2000) addressed the linguistic and thematic coherence of Psalms 73–89 in what he called a canonical approach. He showed some significant linguistic patterns in what is a fairly detailed series of close readings. One of his conclusions was that at both ends the group can be linked closely to the preceding and succeeding books; otherwise, he finds important evidence of interrelations between the psalms in this set. The findings are not, however, interpreted in terms of the context of the fall of Jerusalem in any detail, and links to texts outwith the Psalms are – disappointingly – rather few. What this work provides is more of a database for future work than a thoroughgoing group analysis of the kind we have looked at already. Given the fairly obvious similarities with certain sections of Jeremiah and with Lamentations, and the use made by one of these psalms in a similar context in Maccabees, Cole's book represents perhaps something of a missed opportunity. I shall comment further in the next chapter on the way that this section of the Psalter might fit into the whole; in the meantime it may be sufficient to observe that several psalms within Book III have often been linked with the experience of the destruction of the temple in 587 BCE. While only one of these psalms – 86 – is entitled 'A prayer of David', Cole (2000: 136) suggests a motivation on the part of the editor to ensure that the Davidic covenant was embedded in these otherwise non-Davidic Psalms: 'While Ps. 86 is well integrated into the context of surrounding psalms, the name 'David' still stands as unique in the titles of Book III. No doubt there existed a desire to maintain in the forefront the eschatological and messianic emphasis that is evident across the canonical Psalter.' The concluding psalm in the group reflects on the past promises to David which now appear to have been abandoned or abrogated. Thus 89.38-9:

> But now you have spurned and rejected him;
>> you are full of wrath against your anointed.
> You have renounced the covenant with your servant
>> you have defiled his crown in the dust.

The psalm continues in similar vein, concluding (thus also concluding Book III) with the far from hopeful sentiments:

> Lord, where is your steadfast love of old,
>> which by your faithfulness you swore to David?
> Remember, O Lord, how your servant is taunted;
>> how I bear in my bosom the insults of the peoples,
> with which your enemies taunt, O Lord,
>> with which they taunted the footsteps of your anointed.

Given the other indications of links between Book III and the circumstances of 587 BCE, this sombre assessment of the failure of the Davidic experiment and the sad acceptance of God's withdrawal from his anointed servant serves as a fitting conclusion to this memorial of one of the darkest periods in the history of Israel and Judah.

In respect of Book IV, one study should be noted, an analysis of Psalms 93–100 by David Howard (1997). Like Cole's on Book III, the bulk of Howard's monograph is concerned with a detailed examination of each individual psalm, though with a particular interest in identifying shared language, themes and motifs. His study reinforces the general principle which this chapter has been elucidating, that there is more coherence to sequences of psalms than was once thought. Thus he concludes that 'Psalms 93–100 form a logically coherent unit of community psalms, all concerned with

Yahweh's kingship in one way or another. They probably did not exist as a separate collection after the fashion of Pss. 120–134, but a clear pattern to the thought progression among the psalms is visible.' He goes on to note that his 'study confirms the judgment of many scholars that the Kingship of YHWH psalms are the climax to which the Psalter builds throughout Books I–III' (Howard 1997: 183).

4. Psalms of David

Because of the traditional association of David with the whole of the Psalter, relatively little attention has been paid to *groups* of 'Davidic' psalms. Undoubtedly we need to be suspicious about the authenticity of such attributions and agnostic about their meaning, in particular where we are dealing with psalms in Books IV and V. The greatest density of Davidic psalms is in the first two books (54 out of 72, or 75%). There is just one in Book III (6%) and there are two in Book IV (12%) – a pattern which could easily be reconciled with the idea of an early, possibly authentic tradition which ends at an obvious point: with the psalms of Book III which memorialize the fall of Jerusalem. However, perhaps to our surprise, within the 44 psalms in Book V there are two small groups (108–10 and 138–45) which together constitute 25% of the total; further to which three of the Psalms of Ascents, perhaps randomly, are also attributed to David, thus increasing the overall proportion to 32%. It is important not to make too much of mere numbers, but there is an interesting correlation to be made with one of the most important psalms scrolls from Qumran, which Peter Flint (1997: 192) has identified as being quite deliberately constructed in keeping with a major emphasis on the role and character of David. 11QPs^a is a substantial scroll, containing originally 56 compositions of which 48 are drawn from Books IV and V, and the remainder from other known and otherwise unattested sources. The reordering of psalms and the incorporation of additional pieces displays a 'strong Davidic character', so that 'by dispersing titled Davidic Psalms among untitled ones, the compiler of 11QPs^a has succeeded in permeating the entire collection with a Davidic character and giving "orphan" Psalms a Davidic home'(1997: 193–94). Interestingly, Flint concludes that this scroll, while undoubtedly *copied* at Qumran, 'was almost certainly compiled prior to the Qumran period and is representative of more widespread groups for whom the solar calendar was authoritative' (1997: 201). He argues that the scroll is structured around a 52-week period, which fits with the solar calendar evidenced in the *Book of Jubilees*, a work itself highly regarded at Qumran (1997: 192–93). This might well reflect something which I argued for in my own study of the Psalms of Ascent – a late, perhaps Hasmonaean, emphasis on the messianic significance of David and his association with a Jerusalem reconfigured as the more mystically designated Zion.

The one concentrated study of a group of Davidic psalms is that of Goulder (1990), in which, in his characteristic style, he postulates a processional around Jerusalem in which the Davidic psalms of Book II are linked with key episodes in the king's life. Specifically, he expounds the thesis that in various ways these psalms constitute a liturgical procession in Jerusalem on one day during the autumn festival. They are linked by various clues to the period in David's life 'from the Uriah incident [it seems a little coy to use the word 'incident' to refer to David's having arranged the inevitable death of Uriah in order to marry his widow!] to David's abdication in Solomon's favour'. Embedded in this sequence of psalms is a series of readings from that part of Samuel–Kings which is often referred to as the Succession Narrative, indicated by the placing of 'selah' at the required points in the Psalms text (1990: 28). This certainly fits neatly with his two other studies dealing with Korah and Asaph; however, the same reservations must be entered, the more so in the light of a growing historical and archaeological doubt about the historicity of the David–Solomon period. For if these stories owe more to later imagination than to historical fact, the likelihood that Psalms 51–72 can be explained as Goulder wishes is correspondingly reduced. A contrary indication is, of course, the Tel Dan inscription which refers to the 'house of David', and which would seem at least to support the existence of a dynastic name by some time in the ninth century. The relevant part of the inscription, which dates from the mid- to late-ninth-century BCE, reads (text in square brackets represents damage or gaps in the original):

[I killed Jeho]ram son of [Ahab] king of Israel, and [I] killed [Ahaz]iahu son of [Jehoram kin]g of the House of David. And I set [their towns into ruins and turned] their land into [desolation]. (Finkelstein and Silberman 2002: 129)

The significance of David for the earlier psalms remains somewhat unclear; what is more certain is that at some point in the period from 500 to 100 BCE a definite messianic reading emerged and came, in some circumstances, to dominate. This probably explains the resurgence of attributions to David in Books IV and V, and is, as we shall now see, an important factor in the major Psalms scroll from Qumran.

5. The Qumran Psalms

Undoubtedly the sect behind the Dead Sea Scrolls took a particularly interest in the Psalms. The number of fragments of that book which have turned up, together with major collections like 11QPs[a], shows without doubt that the songs and prayers of Israel were of great significance to them. Moreover, as Sanders, Flint and others have argued, the diverse nature of these collections raises important questions about the status of the traditional Masoretic psalter. At the very least they testify to an important variant development; more probably they show that what we think of now as the psalter was open to considerable change until a relatively late date. To cut short a much longer argument, the fact that Books I–III are found among the Dead Sea texts in much the same form as in the Masoretic text, while Books IV and V vary considerably, strengthens the hypothesis of stages of development. I shall return to this matter when we look at redaction of the Psalter in Chapter 3.

The fragmentary nature of much of the Qumran evidence makes it difficult to use; undoubtedly distinctive ordering is present, and the use of psalms which did not reach the canonical version. However, one sizeable scroll, 11QPs[a], allows us to speculate on firmer ground. Here I am indebted to the ground-breaking work of Peter Flint, which, though dauntingly technical, represents an important advance in our understanding of the development of the Psalms both theologically and liturgically in late intertestamental Judah. We have already noted Flint's proposals about the Davidic nature of this text; his broader conclusion, that at Qumran we find convincing evidence of a fluid situation rather than a minority voice diverging from an already settled mainstream, is presented with a wealth of technical detail. The original suggestions in relation to the significance of this material were made by James Sanders (1967). Sanders faced considerable opposition to his theories; it is pleasing now to see that they have been strongly supported, if not completely vindicated. Whatever our conclusions about the Dead Sea Psalms material, one thing is certain: that the urge to form significant groups around either theological or liturgical themes is well developed. There is, I would argue, no reason to doubt that similar processes were natural to the editors, composers, collectors and users of psalms in the mainstream temple. Thus the Qumran material, far from being the eccentric work of an isolated sect, can be seen as part of a firmly established tradition. Perhaps the thesis, which some have advanced, that those who founded Qumran were part of, or closely related to a Jerusalem sect, helps us to understand the closeness of the relationship between the authorities in the temple and the sectaries by the Dead Sea, at least in their use of the Psalms.

Two very useful publications should be noted for those who are interested to look more closely at the Dead Sea Scrolls evidence. One is the *Dead Sea Scrolls Bible* (Abegg *et al.* 1999) which presents all the biblical books from these sources in the same order as in the Old Testament. The Psalms in particular are to be found on pp. 506–89. The other is the most recent edition of Vermes's *Complete Dead Sea Scrolls in English* (1997), which presents, in complementary fashion, the non-biblical texts. Of particular interest are two non-biblical psalms collections: a series of thanksgiving hymns (1997: 243–300) and the 'Psalms for the Holocaust of the Sabbath' (1997: 321–30). In different ways, both of these testify to the lively and contemporary composition of psalms in a liturgical context at a very late period.

6. Syriac Psalms

Finally we must note, without delaying long, the Syriac apocryphal psalms. The Syriac churches used the Psalms in worship, as did other churches, making their own editions with some characteristic titles differing from those used either in the Masoretic text or the Septuagint. Within this tradition there is to be found a small group of five apocryphal compositions, known since the eighteenth century, and normally numbered 151–55. Psalm 151 has long been known from its presence at the end of the Septuagint Psalter; subsequently Psalms 151 (in two parts); 154; and 155 were identified in the Psalms scroll 11QPs[a]. A useful account of the Syriac tradition is provided by van Rooy (2005).

Other studies of the Psalms of Ascents

Armfield, H.T.

   1874   *The Gradual Psalms: A Treatise on the Fifteen Songs of Degrees with Commentary* (London: J.T. Hayes).

Bovet, Félix.

   1889   *Les Psaumes de Maaloth: Essai d'Explication* (Paris: Neuchatel).

Cox, Samuel.

   1874   *The Pilgrim Psalms: An Exposition of the Songs of Degrees* (London: Daldy, Ibister).

Grossberg, D.
    1989   *Centripetal and Centrifugal Structures in Biblical Poetry: 120–134* (Atlanta: Scholars Press).

Luther, Martin.
    1577 [1899] *A Commentary on the Psalms Called the Psalms of Degrees* (trans. Henry Bull; London: Thomas Vautroullier; reprint, London: W. Simpkin and R. Marshall).

Seybold, Klaus.
    1978   *Die Wallfahrtspsalmen: Studien zur Entstehungsgeschichte von Psalm 120–134* (Neukirchen-Vluyn: Neukirchener Verlag).

Watkins, A.C.
    1899   *The Pilgrim Psalms: being a rendering into English of fifteen Hebrew lyrics, with an essay and some explanations* (Hannibal, NY: A. C. Watkins).

Chapter 3

Historical-Critical Approaches

1. Overview of critical methods in relation to the Psalms

The decisions reached by the various scholars who have approached the Psalms as coherently ordered groups, and whose work we have reviewed in Chapter 2, are to a degree informed by a set of technical approaches: namely the historical-critical methods known as source-, redaction-, tradition- and form-criticism. A good general introduction to methods of biblical criticism is John Barton's *Reading the Old Testament: Method in Biblical Study* (1996). Somewhat older, but still useful are: Norman Perrin's *What is Redaction Criticism?* (1970) and Edgar V. McKnight's *The Bible and the Reader: An Introduction to Literary Criticism* (1985). These methods were first developed to facilitate our understanding of the complex strands of tradition which go to make up the Pentateuch, the historical books and, to a lesser extent, the prophets. In each of these there is a clear case to be made that different writers, different traditions, perhaps even different texts were combined to create the text as we know it. Source criticism used various techniques to spot different writers and writing styles; redaction criticism focused on the work of the editors, who were assumed to have done the work of composition; tradition criticism attempted to tease out possible oral processes (such as folk tales or cultic narratives linked to sanctuaries) which might have helped to bring diverse materials together; and form criticism attempted, by defining the genre of individual passages, to recover possible historical settings in which the text unit in question might have originally functioned. These critical methods inspired a considerable body of highly technical work which produced many interesting results and virtuoso analyses. The so-called Documentary Hypothesis, though now rather out of fashion, was in its essence a triumph of scholarly literary archaeology. While few now endorse its full findings in the terms in which they were originally set out (a series of literary works – J, E, D and P – edited by ancient 'scholars' to form the Pentateuch as we know it), the underlying insights are still valid, and no-one would now seriously question the existence of a complex series of foundations underlying the structure which reached more or less its final form round about 400 BCE.

Whether and how these methods can be deployed in the study of the Psalms is more controversial. Individual psalms do not respond well to source and redaction criticism, and the few attempts to divide up certain pieces on such grounds are now rarely endorsed. Indeed, one of the most striking results of source analysis is the confirmation that Psalms 9 and 10 form a single composition – a conclusion long ago anticipated by the Septuagint numbering of the Psalms, which indeed considers them to be one. Three factors contribute to this conclusion (apart from the Septuagint testimony and the absence of a separate title for Psalm 10): the fact that a fractured, but easily discernible alphabetical acrostic runs through the two psalms; the presence of shared idiosyncratic vocabulary; and the presence of a refrain ('Arise, O Lord') in both psalms. A. A. Anderson (1972: I, 104) also notes that since the presence of *selah* at the end of Psalm 9 is the only example of such a placing, this might further support the claim to unity. Psalm 24 has sometimes been regarded as two separate poems combined; thus Briggs and Briggs (1907: 212): 'Ps. 24 combines two Pss., originally independent, in the one theme'. However, as my own analysis shows (Hunter 1999: 202–03), this is a rather superficial interpretation which ignores a series of linking features. Anderson (1972: I, 200) notes that '[a]lthough the Psalm consists of three distinctive elements, it may well be a literary unity', a judgement with which other recent commentaries concur. More likely candidates for possible separation are 19 and 127. Briggs and Briggs (1907: 162) are clear that 'Ps. 19 is composed of two originally separate poems'; Anderson (1972: I, 167) is in broad agreement. While there is more of a consensus in this case, the most recent view seems to be either a reluctant agreement which underplays its significance (Clifford 2002: 111), or a direct rejection: 'Many modern critics maintain that Psalm 19 is composed of two elements independent of each other ... Such a view, at first sight quite attractive, is not probable, for the strophic structure is so startlingly regular ... that an analysis of the poem in its entirety imposes a different conjecture of its unity' (Terrien 2003: 208)

The pattern of opinion regarding Psalm 127 is similar. An unambiguous assertion that it is composite (Briggs and Briggs 1909: 457) is followed by an expression of dubiety by Anderson (1972: II,

866) which is representative of most recent scholarship (e.g. Allen (1983: 179–80) and Terrien (2003: 829)). There are of course some examples of internal repetition. Thus Psalm 53 more or less faithfully copies 14 (or *vice versa*: the chronology is impossible to determine); Ps. 144.1-7 seems to be a patchwork of phrases from other psalms, as does Psalm 86; 57 and 60 quote extensively from 108; and Psalm 70 is a repetition of Ps. 40.13-17. A more promising direction for the deployment of source criticism is in the exploration of linguistic and semantic links among the members of groups of psalms, where it forms part of the evidence for coherent composition and/or organization. The Psalms of Ascents illustrate this most powerfully, but not exclusively, as the work in particular of Goulder (1996) and Nasuti (1988) on the Psalms of Asaph shows.

A slightly different picture emerges, however, when we turn to the question of redaction criticism. There are undoubtedly several features of the book of Psalms which suggest strongly some kind of editorial intervention. The most obvious of these is the variety of titles used (which, of course, we have already considered under the heading of 'Groups of Psalms' in Chapter 2), and the traditional division into five books which is supported by a series of doxologies at the end of the psalms which close the first four books. These are similar, though not identical, as we can see from Table 3.1.

Table 3.1

Psalm 41.13	Psalm 72.18-19	Psalm 89.52	Psalm 106.48
Blessed be the Lord, the God of Israel,	Blessed be the Lord, the God of Israel, who alone does wondrous things. Blessed be his glorious name	Blessed be the Lord	Blessed be the Lord, the God of Israel,
from everlasting to everlasting.	for ever; may his glory fill the whole earth.	for ever.	from everlasting to everlasting.
Amen and amen.	Amen and amen.	Amen and amen.	And let all the people say, 'Amen.' Praise the Lord!

Table 3.1 (continued)

Psalm 41.13	Psalm 72.18-19	Psalm 89.52	Psalm 106.48
	[72.20 adds: 'The prayers of David son of Jesse are ended.']		[It could be argued that the last phrase, 'Praise the Lord!', ought to be considered as the opening of Psalm 107.]

In addition there is at the end of Book II a separate note, 'The prayers of David son of Jesse are ended', which must surely have some editorial significance. Other evidence of an editorial nature is to be found in the variant headings and numberings in the Septuagint version, which represent ancient alternatives, and the Psalms texts from Qumran in which strikingly different arrangements of psalms are found. Whether these are secondary to, or a contemporary alternative to, the so-called Masoretic Text which lies behind all modern editions is a matter of dispute; that these texts must be taken into account is not contentious. One interesting, if somewhat restricted exploration of this approach is to be found in deClaissé-Walford's *Reading from the Beginning* (1997) in which the author seeks to show the editorial significance of the psalms which begin and end each book. She understands the shape, if not all of the content of the Psalter to have been the ongoing work of the post-exilic community – a work which may not have been finally completed until the first century CE (1997: 105). The book which results ends with a powerful expression of praise, in Psalm 150. deClaissé-Walford concludes (1997: 103):

> But this 'unfettered' praise is only possible at the *end* of the story of the Psalter. The postexilic community must understand where it has come from (the 'Who are we?') and where it is going (the 'What are we to do?') before it can participate in the praise of YHWH the king. Thus the story of the Psalter becomes a story of survival in the changed and changing world with which the postexilic Israelite community is confronted.

The final methodological approach is that of form criticism, which was of course greatly influenced by the pioneering work of Hermann Gunkel. It has been, since the publication of his foundational work, the single most commonly adopted taxonomic technique for psalms study. Unfortunately it has to some extent become an end in itself, rather than – as Gunkel intended – a tool for the recovery of ancient context and use. As we noted in the overview in Chapter 1, too often commentaries seem content to list forms without discussing further the purpose of making such identifications. This can be confusing for novice readers not up to speed on the relevant conventions; more seriously, it leaves the discussion of individual psalms bereft of depth and significance. I shall have more to say on this topic shortly, when we look at these approaches in greater detail.

First, however, I want to introduce a further topic which belongs, I feel, with this set of approaches: namely, the history of the reception of the Psalms. This is a subject which, armed with suitably daunting German titles (*Recepzionsgeschichte* or *Wirkungsgeschichte*: in English, Reception History), has become something of a fashion in recent years. At least two major series are devoted to this approach: Blackwell Bible Commentaries (their web page http://www. bbibcomm.net/reference/guidelines.html gives further information) and Walter de Gruyter's *Encyclopedia of the Bible and its Reception* (publication is still in the future; see http://www.degruyter.com/ rs/5753_8635_ENU_h.htm for more information). It has the distinct advantage of foregrounding such interpretations as those of the early Christian Fathers (*sic*), the mediaeval Rabbis, and the leaders of the Reformation. It is likely that commentaries of this kind will provide a much more generous and imaginative set of readings than we are accustomed to in our somewhat confined denominational or academic contexts. Unfortunately, at the time of writing, none has yet been published. My own chapters on poetry and literature and on liturgy in this volume provide some limited pointers in this direction, but do not attempt to look at the long history of commentary and theological interpretation. In the interests of paying due respect, however, I would like to mention one now almost forgotten book, Prothero's *The Psalms in Human Life* (1914), which contains a series of episodes from history where the psalms played a significant part. One which I particularly warm to concerns an Edinburgh rabble seeing off the local laird's militia by means of a congregational singing of the metrical version of Psalm 124. The account is worth quoting in full (1914: 256):

> Among the staunchest champions of the Presbyterian cause was John Durie, Minister first at Leith, then in Edinburgh. He had been suspended for his plain speaking against the Duke of Lennox. But in 1592 he returned to his 'awin flok of Edinbruche.' The whole town gathered to meet him at the Netherbow Port, and 'goeing upe the streit, with bear heads and laud voices, sang to the praise of God, and testifeing of grait joy and consolation,

the 124th Psalm, "Now Israel may say, and that trewlie," etc., till heavin and erthe resonndit.' So determined was the attitude of the vast concourse of people, that the duke, when he heard the noise and saw the crowd, tore his beard for anger, and hastened out of the city.

Would that today's demonstrators could so easily see off the forces of repressive governments!

2. Redaction and tradition

a. The five book structure: Redaction of the Psalter

The late Gerald Wilson's now classic study (1985) initiated – and still dominates – the recent interest in editorial aspects of the Psalms as a book. He made a convincing case for the collator's use of titles and key phrases to mark off the sections of the Psalter and offered along with this a tentative explanation of the significance of the book as it now is. Wilson argued, on the basis of Mesopotamian and Dead Sea Scrolls exemplars, that titles and introductions were a relevant part of the shaping process, and that (re-)organization of existing material did in fact take place. He concluded that the division into five books was a real editorially induced feature, and that in various ways author and genre headings were used to separate and bind groups of psalms. Where superscriptions are missing, other phenomena (such as the phrases 'Halleluyah' and 'Give thanks' in Books IV and V) serve a similar function. Further suggestions were made by Wilson and others in a collection of essays edited by McCann (1993a). In the most general terms, if Book III deals with the effects of the destruction of the temple and the exile, as many agree, there is something to be said for reading Books I and II in the light of the Judaean monarchy, and Books IV and V as true compositions of the so-called 'second temple'. The latter phrase is a conventional way of alluding to the whole period from the return from exile initiated in Cyrus's reign (535 BCE) to the Roman defeat of the rebel Judaeans in 70 CE; an era, in short, when kingship was largely a theological and messianic ideal, with the exception of the brief Hasmonaean dynasty which may itself, as I have argued (Hunter 1999: 247–48), have taken on some of the clothing of this post-exilic theme. Thus the Psalter as a whole can be given a chiastic structure of the form

Pre-exilic monarchy :: Lament for lost Jerusalem :: Post-exilic messianism

These are to be understood in very broad terms, in that we should not suppose that every psalm in Books IV and V is messianic, nor that every psalm in Books I and II deals directly with the Jerusalem monarchy whose eponymous dynast is David. I assume throughout that Psalms 1 and 2 form an introduction to the whole Psalter, and that their dates of composition and provenance should be considered quite separately from the true beginning of Book I. This is an assumption almost universally held. See, for example, deClaissé-Walford (1997: 37-41).

It is worth exploring this structure in more detail, since it seems to ignore (or rather, to pre-empt) the fivefold division, and it appears at first sight to have historical significance. The origins of the fivefold structure are quite unclear, though some clues can be identified. Thus, for example, the extra concluding notice in Ps. 72.20, 'The prayers of David son of Jesse are ended', might have afforded a rather simple division at the point when the laments of what is now Book III were added to an already existing collection. Continuing this speculative theme, we note further that of all the supposed doxologies the one at the end of Book III is the simplest: 'Blessed be the Lord for ever. Amen and amen.' Thus two quite straightforward markers serve to define first of all a bipartite Psalter in which a Davidic collection is followed by an exilic 'update' in the form of Psalms 73–89. To this were then added, as part of the post-exilic liturgical process, various groups of psalms tailored to its own needs: the festivals of Pesach, Shevuot and Sukkot (cf. Psalms 113–18); the growing sense of a messianic ideal which would in the fullness of time 'restore the fortunes of Zion' (in the words of Ps. 126.1, which echo the prayer from Book III found in Ps. 85.4); the possible use of Psalms 120–32 in an autumn festival; and the central importance of Torah (Psalm 119). These are, by the way, only representative selections. The introduction of the doxology at the end of Psalm 89 would be an indication of this stage of development.

If this analysis is plausible, there needs to be a further proposal as to why and how the subdivision into five books took place. I note first that the two doxologies which effect this further partition are the most like each other, sharing a very specific phrasing: 'Blessed be the Lord, the God of Israel, from everlasting to everlasting.' It is interesting that this formula, which continues to be a liturgical expression in the synagogue, appears in 1 Chron. 29.10-13, a striking passage which bears comparison with the Jewish prayer that in all probability lay at the heart of what Christians know as 'the Lord's Prayer'. A comparison of the psalms doxology, the Chronicles prayer, and the Lord's Prayer, is set out in Table 3.2. The purpose of this comparison is not to suggest any direct dependence, but rather to illustrate a more modest contention: that certain formulations were well known from liturgies in actual use, and might be expected to turn up in a variety of contexts. An earlier example of the same phenomenon is to be found in the two silver amulets discovered in Jerusalem and datable to the late seventh or early sixth centuries, on which the text of Num. 6.24-26 was inscribed. This passage, often referred to as the Aaronic blessing, is a striking liturgical fragment, and its discovery on these amulets is testimony not to the biblical text of Numbers, but to the probability that it had a prominent place in a liturgy of the time.

Table 3.2

Psalms 41.13, 106.48	1 Chronicles 29.10b-13	Matthew 6.9b-13
Blessed be the Lord, the God of Israel,	Blessed are you, O Lord the God of Israel, our Father	2. hallowed be your name
from everlasting to everlasting.	from everlasting to everlasting.	1. Our Father in heaven 9. *for ever, Amen.*
	Yours, O Lord, are the greatness, the power, the glory, the victory, and the majesty;	8. *For the kingdom and the power and the glory are yours*
	for all that is in the heavens and on the earth is yours;	4. your will be done on earth as it is in heaven
	yours is the kingdom, O Lord,	3. your kingdom come
	and you are exalted as head above all	
		5. Give us this day our daily bread.
		6. And forgive us our debts, as we also have forgiven our debtors.
		7. And do not bring us to the time of trial, but rescue us from the evil one.

Note: I have included (using italics) the addition which is commonly used, and is found in a number of ancient mss. The text is ordered to show links with Chronicles.

1 Chronicles 28–29 deals with the transfer of power from the dying David to his chosen successor, Solomon, in a formal setting. The corresponding passage in Samuel–Kings is 1 Kgs. 1.32–2.12; and though this is one of those places where the Chronicler clearly departs from the earlier source, it makes sense to pair them in terms of their chronological position in the history of David and Solomon. There is, in 1 Kgs 1.48, a blessing uttered by David which opens with similar words to those in 1 Chron. 29.10: 'Blessed be the Lord, the God of Israel', and then goes on to celebrate God's provision of Solomon as David's heir. The Kings formulation is simpler, and less liturgically defined than that in Chronicles.

One further piece in this jigsaw is the citation of Ps. 106.47-48 in 1 Chron. 16.35-36. The use by Chronicles of various psalms from Books IV and V could be the subject of a more extensive discussion, and will be discussed further in Chapter 5; for the moment I simply want to note this as evidence for the existence of the doxology at the end of Book IV by some time in the fourth century.

Putting the various pieces together provides us with an attractive hypothesis: a collection of hymns and songs represented by Psalms 3–72 was at some point expanded by the addition of Psalms 73–89, and this is indicated by the final notice in Psalm 72. In all probability the simple doxology which is now found in Ps. 89.52 marked the end of that expanded collection. Then, in the period of the revival of the temple under the auspices of the Babylonian Jewish cadre represented by Ezra and Nehemiah, further materials were composed and found their way into a now further expanded collection. On the evidence of the Qumran Psalms materials, this expansion was quite inconsistent, and depended on the interests of different sects or traditions. This led to a *de facto* threefold volume (pre-exilic, exile lamentations, and post-exilic) along the lines indicated above; however, it is not likely that this was ever formally recognized. I would suggest that, with the new emphasis on Torah as the heart of the religion of the Jews, the second-temple community at some point in time took advantage of the limited subdivisions indicated in Psalms 72 and 89 to impose a more systematic division into five books, mirroring (as has sometimes been suggested) the five books of Torah, but without attempting to make any thematic links. This is why attempts to match the contents of the five books of psalms with the Pentateuch have failed to be persuasive, though in support of this contention, we may point to the dominating presence of the grand acrostic Psalm 119. Further indicative evidence is to be found in the presence in Chronicles of an emergent liturgical formula whose full expression seems to belong to the fourth century or later (it is absent from Kings), and which is used to demarcate the five-book Psalter.

b. The problem of pre-exilic compositions and oral tradition

It is almost always assumed that the oldest psalms go back to the period of the monarchy – or monarchies – with some sharing features in common with certain Ugaritic compositions. The chief proponent of close links between Ugaritic and the language of the psalms was Mitchell Dahood, who worked on the grammatical consequences in detail in his three-volume commentary (1970). It is now rarely claimed that any psalms are directly linked to Ugarit, a city which fell into ruin before any identifiable Israelite settlement came into being; what is more plausibly argued is that these sources exemplify a more general Canaanite tradition which would certainly have been familiar to the people of Israel and Judah. Thus it is recognized that there is continuity of language, of style, and to some extent of religious belief, cultic practice, and mythic thought-world, between Israel and Judah on the one hand, and Canaan on the other. Jonathan Tubb's *Canaanites* (2006) provides a balanced and readable presentation of the cultures of Canaan from the Bronze Age to the Iron Age. Tubb makes it clear that the story (including that of Israel) is one predominantly of continuity of both people and cultures. References in the scholarly literature to the monarchic period, particularly in relation to the Psalms, usually have in mind either the 'united' kingdom of David and Solomon or the subsequent kingdom of Judah centred on the city of Jerusalem and the Temple. An exception is to be found in Goulder's argument for the (northern) Israelite provenance of the Psalms of the Sons of Korah; but the pattern I have identified is, I think, broadly accurate. Within these general terms of reference the question of individual authorship is commonly avoided, without any direct denial of some role for David.

Commentaries tend to atomize the Psalter in this respect, examining each individual psalm for its form, linguistic style, and possible historical origins, without much attention to the kind of grouping questions which I have foregrounded. Thus it is not uncommon to find psalms from almost anywhere in the collection identified as 'archaic' (for example, both Psalms 29 and 132), 'pre-exilic' or 'post-exilic' and so on, as though there were reliable objective criteria for such judgements. Now we can certainly agree that the form and style of Psalm 29 has much in common with Canaanite material; but that hardly ensures its antiquity, since it is equally clear that Psalm 96 has similar echoes without being thought to be of ancient provenance. Nor does the fact that Psalm 132 refers to the same ark tradition that we find in 1 Samuel 4–6 and 2 Samuel 6 have necessary chronological implications. I do not want to labour this point: the problem is clear.

But what is less clear is the more general question of *whether* and *how* any pre-exilic compositions might have survived into the liturgy of the second temple. Is it reasonable to propose that any significant body of psalms composed during the period of the monarchy/ies could have survived the catastrophic destruction of Jerusalem?

Let me illustrate with a familiar parallel: the story in 2 Kings 22–23 of the discovery of 'the book of the law' when the temple was being repaired in Josiah's reign. Opinion on the significance of this episode has shifted considerably through the years. In the heyday of the documentary hypothesis it was seen as corroborative evidence for the existence of the D ('Deuteronomistic') document which was often supposed to have originated in Israel, and subsequently brought to Jerusalem in the effects of exiles from the Assyrian destruction. Being of less interest to the temple authorities, it was stored, as it were, in a cupboard until it was brought to light in Josiah's reign. The grounds for this identification are principally that the ideology of the sole legitimacy of the Jerusalem cult and the need to destroy all rivals is central to both Josiah's policy and Deuteronomy.

More sceptical scholars have since cast doubt on this neat coincidence. Apart from the problem of how refugees fleeing from the Assyrians would have had time to collect the necessary materials (clay tablets?), there is a growing sense that the coincidence is in fact the result of a *later* Deuteronomistic school having 'planted' both the story of Josiah's destruction of the high places and the discovery of the mysterious book in order to support their own post-exilic ideology. In defence of this perhaps rather radical reading are, first of all, signs that Deuteronomy reflects the strongly anti-royalist mood of the sixth century, and second, evidence from correspondence from the Jewish colony in Elephantine in Egypt that their 'rival' temple was seen as perfectly in order by the Jerusalem authorities of the period immediately after Josiah. Elephantine was a colony, originally of Jewish mercenaries in the employment of the Egyptian government, which flourished on the island of Yeb, or Elephantine, in the Lower Nile region at the border with Nubia. It was probably founded around 650 BCE; the bulk of the papyri found there date from 495-399 BCE. Thus, what *seemed* pre-exilic may in fact be the (idealized? romanticized? politicized?) work of the period from 535 onwards.

What this brief digression illustrates is the requirement on scholars to be realistic about the material conditions in which texts might have been produced and transmitted, and about the political, theological, or ideological matrix in which they might have flourished. Let me at the outset dispose of the 'oral transmission' mechanism. I have no doubt that memorable liturgical pieces might have circulated in popular awareness, and that (to take the case of Deuteronomy) legends and tales of kings and ancient heroes could have flourished in the popular domain. But the first two books of the Psalter, as we now have them, do not constitute oral material, any more than the highly formalized book of Deuteronomy. The work that has been done on this aspect of the psalms has not reached any very positive conclusions. Thus Robert Culley (1967) carried out a study of possible orality in the psalms based on the oral composition theories of Parry and Lord (for details see Lord (1960)); on his own admission the results were largely negative. Some time later William Watters (1976) examined, with a rather critical eye, earlier work on possible orality in Hebrew poetry, including both formula-based and word-pair-based oral composition, and decided that there was little evidence of this phenomenon in the extant Hebrew poetry.

I have no doubt that hymns were sung in the first temple (which was, in all probability, the royal chapel of the kings of Judah); nor do I doubt that public festivals and ceremonies were performed there. What I do seriously question is the likelihood that anyone other than the professionals was familiar with extensive performance pieces. If these survived, it would have to have been through the agency of these same professionals (priests or Levites seem solid candidates). This is not to discount the persistence of short popular formulae such as those found in the benedictions in Tables 3.1 and 3.2, the Aaronide blessing found in Num. 6.24-26 and on an extant seventh- or sixth-century amulet from Jerusalem, or the ark slogan in Num. 10.35 which might be echoed in Ps. 132.8. But such fragments only serve to confirm the likelihood that nothing more extensive would, in the normal run of things, have survived orally.

Might written collections (inscribed on clay tablets or written on papyrus) have made it through to the second temple period? This is, of course, not impossible: papyrus fragments could have found their way into the baggage of the exiles; clay tablets might have survived the chaos to be recovered in due course when a new generation of temple officials got to work on the restoration of the cult. What does seem unlikely, to the point of vanishing probability, is that anything as systematic as Books I and II was preserved intact. Certainly they did not survive orally, and it is more credible to believe that these opening books represent a considerable expansion and rewriting of whatever limited resources might have been available, possibly inspired by the new 'History of Israel' represented by the appearance of forms of the books of Samuel and Kings by the mid-sixth century. In due course the contents of Book III, perhaps independently composed in memory of the disaster of 587, were combined with these consciously archaizing materials to form, in essence, the first Psalter.

The speculations in the preceding paragraph are less important than the problem they seek to illustrate. We will almost certainly never know for sure how these first three books were carved out of the rubble of the destruction of the temple and the desire for a new beginning; but that lack of certainty does not allow us to resort to the essentially naive assumption that a pre-exilic book of Psalms made the transformation essentially unchanged from the royal chapel of the kings of Judah to the priestly temple of the heirs of Ezra and Nehemiah. I am convinced, in short, that the book of Psalms is both in form, and to a large extent in substance, a post-exilic composition. Some work done recently by Jerome Creach (1996) has raised the possibility that there is a significant distribution of terms for 'refuge' in the Psalter which may reflect editorial input. One of his conclusions – that 'two sections of the Psalter (Pss. 2–72; 90–106) share a wealth of vocabulary and theological interests with two sections of the book of Isaiah (Isa. 1–39; 40–55)' – would have obvious implications for the dating of editorial activity to the post-exilic period (1996: 124).

3. Form criticism

a. Introduction

This is not the place for an exhaustive treatment of the forms of biblical psalms. Many standard introductions, and most commentaries, provide form-critical analysis of individual psalms and, on occasion, lists allocating the whole collection to a taxonomy of types. The ultimate conclusion of this approach is the two volumes by E.S. Gerstenberger (1988, 2001) which give an exhaustive account of the forms of the psalms. The method was originated and developed by Hermann Gunkel, one of the real giants of the discipline of Biblical Studies, and the best place to seek an understanding of what he sought to achieve by this approach is the opening chapter of his *Introduction to the Psalms* (1933 [1998]). For Gunkel, form criticism of the Psalms was directed towards specific ends, and was not a task whose completion justified the commentator in putting down his or her pen with a sigh of relief. On the contrary, he concludes his introduction by remarking that 'a work as comprehensive as the one described above naturally cannot be completed in a single stroke. We must be satisfied to begin the work' (1933 [1998]: 21). This chapter, written towards the end of his life, expresses Gunkel's regrets that relatively few scholars have understood and taken up his methodological approach. He need not have worried, for a review of his programme for Psalms study will strike anyone who knows anything of the discipline over the last seventy years as very familiar indeed. In the interests, then, of paying due respect to a great scholar, and of providing a convenient résumé of form criticism and the Psalms, I will devote most of the rest of this section to a review of Gunkel's own account of his project. Emphases in quotations are present in the 1998 translation.

b. Gunkel's *Introduction to the Psalms*

Gunkel begins by delineating the particular difficulties attendant upon the study of the Psalms as being (a) their terseness and allusiveness, (b) their lack of specific reference, (c) a tendency to hyperbole, (d) the problem of Hebrew tense, (e) the brevity of most individual psalms, (f) the lack of 'almost any credible tradition about the poet, or the reason and times when the songs originated', (g) the condition of the text, which is often damaged and obscure, and (h) the fact that '*no internal ordering principle for the individual psalms has been transmitted for the whole*'. He notes that 'Even the so-called pilgrimage psalms (120–134) are comprised almost exclusively of different genres. Thus no certainty exists in questionable cases, whether a psalm should be understood with its neighbour' (1933 [1998]: 1–3). I have addressed (h) already, in Chapter 2, and it will be clear that for various reasons I do not share Gunkel's view that divergence of genre is a barrier to coherence of order. Some of the other points he makes are, to be sure, a feature of poetry in general (thus (a), (b), (c), and (e)): we do not expect poetry to be factually referential, and its ability to convey highly charged 'packets' of meaning and emotion in short phrases is universal. Points (d) and (g) are somewhat technical, and need not delay us here. For those who have Hebrew, the problem of tenses will be familiar; though it is, in my opinion, a problem which is often exaggerated. It is not strictly true to claim, as some do, that Hebrew has no fixed tenses; and in poetry in any case, whether in Hebrew or other languages, the question of the timeframe or reference of the verse is often deliberately ambiguous. We are, therefore, no worse off in struggling with Hebrew poetry than with any other. Finally, it is certainly correct to note (f) that we have virtually no information about the poets who wrote the Psalms and when they were written. Recent scholarship has shown that similar dubiety attaches to a much wider range of biblical material than was thought in Gunkel's day, and theory over the last half-century has tended in any case to play down, if not to eliminate, the importance of authorship and date. It is interesting, therefore, to find Gunkel himself sounding a remarkably contemporary note in this regard:

> The question with which research has occupied itself to this point is with *assigning a date* to the psalms. One can tell from the position that we generally give it in the investigation that we do not consider this problem to be the most important. Understanding a written work appears far more important to us as the proper and final task behind which all 'criticism' should constantly take a back seat in significance. (1933 [1998]: 21)

It is, of course, a fact that Gunkel had been working on the genres of the Psalms for many years. The chapter I am reviewing here is something of a mature reflection on an already accomplished body of work. He had already delineated the genres he thought relevant to the Psalter; they are:

hymns
psalms of the enthronement of YHWH
communal complaints
royal psalms
individual complaints
individual thanksgiving songs

His purpose in employing this formal taxonomy was in the interest of understanding context. He used a term which has since found a role as a technical expression: setting in life, or *Sitz-im-Leben*, and he hoped that by properly classifying individual psalms he would be able to reach a better understanding of the whole body of poems and songs which makes up the Psalter. Thus he affirmed that

> there is an unbreakable principle of scholarship that nothing can be understood outside of its context. Accordingly, the *particular task of psalm studies should be to rediscover the relationships between the individual songs* that did not occur with the transmission, or that occurred only in part. Once we have coordinated the psalms that belong together internally, we can hope to achieve a precise understanding of the poem by means of a thoroughgoing comparison. (1933 [1998]: 3)

During Gunkel's lifetime the great nineteenth-century discoveries of texts from Egypt and Mesopotamia had added immeasurably to the comparative resources available to biblical scholars. Hymns and cultic texts from Egypt, Babylon and Assyria opened the door to a far more systematic study of ancient Near Eastern poetry than had hitherto been possible, even though the Hittite and the Ugaritic finds and the scrolls from the Dead Sea lay still in the future. Accordingly Gunkel includes in his programme a review of psalms wherever they are found: in narrative books of the Old Testament; in Job; in the prophets; in Lamentations; in the Apocrypha; in the early Christian period; and in Babylonian and Egyptian sources. This is, of course, a collaborative enterprise. No one scholar can hope to be competent, far less expert, in all the relevant disciplines; and what was true even in Gunkel's day is all the more true today. But what lies at the heart of Gunkel's ambition is nothing less than a comprehensive classification of genres, forms and motifs by means of which it will be possible to reach some understanding of the original purpose and setting of the Psalms as part of a wider phenomenon of cultic poetry and song. This is how he puts it:

> Since it concerns literary witnesses, the *genres* of this type of poetry must be substantiated. Accordingly, *genre research* in the Psalms is nonnegotiable, not something one can execute or ignore according to preference. Rather it is the *foundational work* without which there can be no certainty in the remainder. It is the firm ground from which everything else must ascend. (1933[1998]: 5)

Time has served somewhat to dampen his hopes, in that the expectation that lay behind form analysis has not proved to be realizable. There is, for example, too little reliable information about the actual practice of the cult either during the monarchy or in the second temple period. The apparent historical references in the rest of the Old Testament are difficult to date reliably, and it is not always clear whether they represent actuality at some point in time, or an ideal situation (for example, the clearly exaggerated numbers in the Chronicler's account of David's arrangements for the service of the temple). Moreover, the propriety of transferring elements of ritual from Babylon to Jerusalem is not proved. Gunkel is, of course, much more optimistic. Appealing to the work of scholars like W. Robertson Smith, he argues that we can find a wealth of clues in scripture more generally for what took place in worship. He proposes that there is a significant connection between words and actions, for example in 1 Kgs 13.15ff.; Num. 21.17; Jer. 51.59ff.; Num. 6.24ff.; Deut. 21.7; and so on. This implies that 'Israel's worship service was once very full of these cultic speeches. One gains this impression even more strongly from the Babylonian worship service' (1933 [1998]: 10). He identifies, for example, 'songs of summons' in Num. 10.35f., and in Ps. 24.7ff. His method is eclectic – a problem which we shall encounter again in the work of Mowinckel (1962) and Johnson (1955 [1962]). Thus, to discover the character of the 'thanksgiving offering' he brings together the cup of salvation in Ps. 116.13, dancing round the altar in Ps. 118.27, a festival procession in Ps. 42.5, a location at the entrance to the temple in Ps. 118.19, expressions of joy and the use of music in Isa. 30.29, and the possibility of a vigil in Ps. 134.1 (1933 [1998]: 10–13 *passim*).We shall return to some of these questions in Chapter Five.

As to the methodology itself, Gunkel is remarkably explicit. He starts with a question, to which he provides his unequivocal answer:

> *So where would the poetry of the Psalms have had its 'setting in life?'*
> Judaism would have performed the poetry in its cult. ... Even now, the biblical Psalms are used by the synagogue and the Christian church in the original text, in translation, and in paraphrase. Thus, we may dare to presume that they also arose in the cult of Israel originally. This supposition is then immediately confirmed by an observation that no observant reader of the psalter can deny, specifically the *formal nature* of many, though not all, of these poems. (1933 [1998]: 7)

It is, of course, a commonplace that not all psalms have a public or cultic purpose. Some are quite clearly personal or reflective, probably a consequence of the development of the genre from that of public ceremony to private meditation. Gunkel recognizes this clearly, though his arguments might strike a modern reader as anthropologically naive. Thus, 'one can expect from the outset, based on the general path of the history of religion, that the "cult poems" are older while the "spiritual songs" – as we call the poems that really demonstrate the personal life – represent a later developmental stage' (1933 [1998]: 13). It is the essentially cultic songs that form the basis of Gunkel's project – though we might, with hindsight, enter a caveat to the effect that it is not as straightforward as he might have imagined to distinguish the two. Consider, for example, Psalm 2, which most traditional genre analyses construe as a coronation psalm. Many, indeed, see it as having once had a part to play in the enthronement ceremonial in Judah. But, as it now stands, Psalm 2 forms a messianic introduction, in tandem with Psalm 1, to the Psalter as a whole. It is not clear, therefore, whether it represents a genuinely ancient piece re-deployed, or a pastiche created to set the tone for a post-exilic theological reading of the Psalms. This is an example of the circularity of argument which endangers the form-critical project; for the judgement as to whether a piece is original to its apparent setting, or an imitation of some kind, is itself a historical one which somewhat pre-empts the use of the methodology as a quest for original settings.

Gunkel goes on to set out a framework for the study of the Psalms which has remained the practical norm for much continuing work since. The first task is to delineate the genres of the Psalms. This must be done carefully, according to a number of criteria, which he specifies as follows:

(a)   to collect together only 'those poems which as a group belong to a specific *occasion in the worship service*, or at least derive from one. We must present this cultic occasion as precisely as possible, utilizing the allusions from the numerous sources for this purpose.'

(b)   'those songs belonging together must naturally indicate a common treasury of *thoughts and moods*. These are the ones which were provided by their [*Sitz-im-Leben*], or which could easily be attached to it.'

(c)   It is 'absolutely necessary ... that all of the individual pieces belonging to the genre should indeed be associated relatively clearly by their common "language related to the form"'. Interestingly, Gunkel is at pains to deny that form and content can be separated: 'it should be expressly accented that a literary-historical inspection concerns itself not only with the form, but also just as much with *the content* of the poem'. In detail, it will be simple forms and preferred vocabulary that will be analysed. (1933 [1998]: 15–16)

In setting out these guidelines Gunkel is clearly strongly influenced by his anticipated outcome: the delineation of the worship of ancient Israel, with a clarification of which psalms belong where, and why.

The second task is to look more closely at motifs within the various sections of a particular genre. Thus, for example, we might look at a communal lament, and notice the detailed motifs which occur in their introductions (formulae like 'How long, O Lord'), the manner in which the complaint is spelled out and reminiscences of past blessing recorded in the body of the psalm, and the forms which the conclusion may take – such as, for instance, a vow, or a note of thanks for a prayer answered, or a downbeat repetition of the opening lament. By collecting together elements of psalms which contain the same motif in the context of the same genre it will be possible to construct norms and patterns with which to extend the discussion to the Psalter as a whole and to the use made of psalms in worship.

Finally, we can attempt some historical analysis, in which identification of the setting can be used to locate material within the broader history of the cult. But this is not the only purpose of the method. Identifying how the psalms are used is more important than reaching conclusions about when and where they originated. Moreover, part of the task is to study the historical development of the genres themselves. Gunkel regarded shorter psalms as older, and mixed genres in a single psalm as evidence of a more sophisticated development through time; as also the development of pious poetry, and of perceptive reflection, such as the wisdom psalms, which represented 'higher' forms of individual religious experience.

c. Gunkel's types

A great many form-critical studies have followed the work of Gunkel, and much has been done to classify and identify the main genres. The following summary notes the outline structures of the basic types identified by Gunkel, drawn primarily from Gunkel himself, with some help from a useful handbook produced by Claus Westermann (1980: 132–3). It is worth observing that, aside from the elaborate reconstructions offered by Mowinckel and Johnson, the majority of those who have attended to Psalms genres have assumed the existence of a familiar cultic context *a priori* to which they have assigned the Psalms. For all its inbuilt faults, Gunkel's methodology was careful in avoiding this kind of begging of the question; it may be that had more careful attention been paid to what he advocated, better results might have been achieved.

The principal types identified by Gunkel, as noted above, are, together with their identifying motifs:

(a) Hymns (example Psalm 113):
    (i)   call to praise
    (ii)   reasons for praise
         1. the Lord is great
         2. the Lord is good
    (iii) Alleluiah!
(b) Psalms of the enthronement of YHWH
(c) Communal complaints (example Psalm 80):
    (i)   invocation
    (ii)   complaint ('we', 'they', 'you')
    (iii) review of God's past help
    (iv) petition ('hear!', 'turn!', 'intervene!', 'do this!')

    (v)   praise / vow to praise
(d) Royal psalms
(e) Individual complaints (example Psalm 13):
    (i)   invocation
    (ii)   complaint ('I', 'they', 'you')
    (iii) review of God's past help
    (iv) petition ('hear!', 'turn!', 'intervene!', against enemies)
    (v)   praise / vow to praise
(f) Individual thanksgiving songs (example Psalm 30):
    (i)   introduction
         1. summons
         2. initial summary
    (ii)   call to praise
    (iii) account (narrative)
         1. crisis in retrospect
         2. rescue ('I cried', 'You heard', 'You intervened')
    (iv) praise / vow to praise

d. Further work on form: I. Royal psalms

By way of illustration of the directions which the study of form in the psalms has taken I will briefly examine two types of approach in this section: the attempt to define and contextualize the so-called 'royal psalms'; and the use of the psalms of lament to argue for a meaningful theological shape to the Psalter.

In a study first published in 1976, and republished with a bibliographical addendum in 1986, John Eaton gave what can best be described as a maximalist analysis of possible royal psalms and their function in ancient Israel. By 'maximalist' I mean that he regards early dating as non-controversial, and sees the enemy in most of the psalms as external to Israel and therefore appropriate to an interpretation of the subject of the psalms as being the king. Moreover, he wants considerably to expand Gunkel's original set of ten royal psalms (2, 18, 20, 21, 45, 72, 101, 110, 132, 144.1-11) by adding two further sets: 3, 4, 7, 9–10, 17, 22, 23, 27, 28, 35, 40, 41, 57, 59, 61, 62, 63, 66, 69, 70, 71, 75, 89, 91, 92, 94, 108 [with 44, 60, 74, 80, 83, 84], 118, 138, 140, 143, which he regards as clearly royal, and a number of 'less clear cases': 5, 11, 16, 31, 36, 42–43, 51, 52, 54, 55, 56, 73, 77, 86, 102, 109, 116, 120, 121, 139, 141, 142. Eaton has no difficulties with the proposal that the royal liturgies of Israel were similar to those of the surrounding nations, in particular the Mesopotamian *akitu* ceremonies at New Year. The essentials of this festival involved the 'disappearance' and ritual humiliation of the king, before a dramatic restoration and revival of his office, symbolic of the cleansing of the community and the restoration of Marduk to his position as supreme deity in Babylon. A setting of this kind for the Israelite autumn festival, argued for by both Gunkel and Mowinckel, and used by Johnson in his famous study of 'sacral kingship' (1955), is accepted, and Eaton concludes that Johnson's position is

> in the main more satisfactory than that of Mowinckel. Firstly a survey of Gunkel's 'royal psalms' pointed to this conclusion ... and secondly we have found that the extra psalms of the king add valuable corroboration. With reasonable clarity we see that the dramatic celebration of Yahweh's kingship in the autumn festival entailed also a dramatic presentation of the Davidic office. In symbol the king was beset by enemies from all quarters and brought to the realm of death; his humble fidelity was thus proved and Yahweh answered his prayer, exalting him above all dangers and foes. While the order of the ceremonies and texts remains uncertain, the chief elements of the royal suffering and exaltation are strongly attested, as is also the close relation to the assertion of Yahweh's own kingship. (Eaton 1986: 133)

Eaton concludes by describing a set of 27 characteristics, supposedly identifiable in the royal psalms, which present us with an ideal for the office of the king as delineated by the Psalms. The list is too long to repeat here: it is to be found in Eaton (1986: 135–97).

Many questions are begged by a study such as this, leading to a pronounced circularity of argument. Eaton deploys the Deuteronomistic history in Samuel and Kings in a rather uncritical fashion, and does not really go beyond the mere assertion that the kings of Israel and Judah (whoever they were) had associated with them a body of liturgical psalms. With these prior assumptions in place, the quest for royal psalms is flawed, since it simply reads back into the Psalter an already determined position about their existence and their function in the royal cults of Israel and Judah. The circularity becomes most pronounced when, as in Eaton's study, the long list of 'royal' psalms – which have been selected and defined as such because of the prior assumption of royal use – is then used to define and describe the ritual role of the king. A recent monograph by Scott Starbuck (1999) takes a much more sceptical (or minimalist) view of the royal psalms. Starbuck reviews the various scholarly positions on kingship and the Psalms, highlighting in particular the difference between, on the one hand, those who use psalms to describe the office of the king and, on the other, those who derive from them an account of the king's participation in the cult. The latter include the 'myth and ritual' school which sought in such bodies of literature as the Psalms the text or 'myth' which supposedly accompanied a dramatic ritual. A.R. Johnson is the most significant representative of this movement within Psalms study – a movement, it must be said, which has now largely been rejected. One further, and more recent development should be noted: the argument, advanced in particular by Wilson (1985) and McCann (1993a), that the placing of Gunkel's royal psalms has a decided canonical purpose.

In sharp contrast with earlier studies, Starbuck's findings are decidedly negative. He notes that, unlike supposed Mesopotamian parallels, none of the 'royal' psalms cites historical personages, and even the names of the kings are missing. Nor is there any evidence that they were 'anonymized' for the use of successive kings. He concludes that we do not have enough evidence to reconstruct royal rituals, nor can we assume that these psalms represent 'standardized elements of a royal cult stretching from King David to King Zedekiah'. They were not at the service of the ideology of individual kings. 'Rather, it seems to be the case that RPss focus on the institution of kingship itself' (1999: 99). We must be equally pessimistic about the chances of recovering or reconstructing a kingship-renewal festival; instead, Starbuck offers a revised definition: 'The RPss are psalms whose concern is the institution of Israelite kingship. Their protagonist is an unspecified king; hence he is a typological representative of the "office" of the institution' (1999: 101).

The arguments of those who construe the royal psalms as having a key canonical significance fare little better. They scarcely constitute a *gattung*, being of various different types; there is no evidence that they ever formed a connected subgroup (indeed, some – such as Psalm 45 – were already part of another group; in this case the Korah collection). A few (2; 72; and 89) may well have been carefully placed at the 'seams' of books, but it is more probable that they were selected individually for their suitability than that the editors had access to a special royal collection. The conclusion is that, whatever earlier form or existence they may have had, Gunkel's royal psalms are part now of an exilic move towards the democratization of the royal ideal.

e. Further work on form: II. Psalms of lament

Undoubtedly the Psalms of Lament have inspired a significant body of commentary, not least because of the sense of personal involvement that they inspire. In this section I want to revisit these psalms by addressing Nasuti's interesting rethinking of genre in psalms interpretation (1998), in which he engages in particular with the work of Westermann (1981) and Brueggemann (1980, 1984). On a more traditional basis, Broyles (1989) offers an impressive form-critical and theological study of these psalms in which he identifies distinctive elements of 'plea' and 'protest' and notes, among other things, the real element of cognitive dissonance involved in the preservation and use of a group of psalms which consistently presents a sense of failure, of disappointment, and of unresolved issues with God.

Westermann and Brueggemann have, in work with a more theological focus, interpreted Israel's lament psalms as giving an existential shape to the Psalter as a whole. It will be more appropriate to describe their approach in Chapter 6; for the time being I will restrict my comments to Nasuti's discussion of 1998. Nasuti notes that these two scholars have shifted the significance of form away from Gunkel's original project of *Sitz-im-Leben*. 'For both ... the way one groups the psalms has theological, as well as *religionsgeschichtliche* significance. Such theological interests were not absent in Gunkel, but they were clearly not his dominant concern' (1998: 15). This represents, in fact, a return to the mainstream; and Nasuti illustrates his point by means of an examination of the seven Penitential Psalms (6; 32; 38; 51; 102; 130; 143), which originated as a distinct set in early Christian tradition and were at different times read as a support for faith or as an aid to the mediaeval *imitatio Christi*. The point is that form is not simply a means to recovering a lost setting: what we understand by form is also driven by the questions we put to the Psalter. None of the genres are defined objectively enough to stand alone, independently of the needs of the reader. According to Nasuti, Gunkel's emphasis on setting has morphed, in the hands of scholars like Westermann, into a concern for Israel's specific theological interests, and with Brueggemann (psalms of orientation, disorientation and new orientation) into a setting in human (religious) life as a whole. The case of the Penitential Psalms shows how *setting controls genre* (1998: 45–49).

'All would agree that texts are defined as belonging to a certain genre because such texts are seen to share features in common. What is less acknowledged, however, is that the question of genre is really a question of *which* elements a reader is brought to see as common to certain texts' (1998: 52). In his fourth chapter, Nasuti makes the interesting point that we rarely ask how any particular genre achieves its effect or performs its functions. For example, '*How* do the hymns function as texts of praise, especially for those communities who have been given such texts as examples of canonical or community-authorized prayer? The fact that we tend to assume the answer to such a question shows just how basic this question is' (1998: 84).

It seems that when we ask this question there is a perceptible shift in the direction of theology; perhaps an inevitable move as soon as we accept that form is related to the reader's need for meaning as much as to the cultic setting. Brueggemann, accordingly, proposed three levels of expressive function: to express 'the conscious sentiments of the person praying'; to '"bring to speech" that which is felt, but does not become fully real without the assistance of these texts'; and, deeper still, 'For Brueggemann, at least some of the psalms have the additional function of bringing to expression how life really is' (1998: 85). In a kind of closure of a hermeneutical circle, Nasuti notes that centuries earlier St Athanasius anticipated many of Brueggemann's points, with the addition of the point that the psalms can actually *do* something to a person – they have a sacramental effect (1998: 107–16). We have travelled, it seems, a long way from Gunkel's ground-breaking efforts.

4. Reception of the Psalms

It would be negligent to omit some reference to the way that the Psalms have been received within the long history of their use. To some extent this is covered by what we shall have to say about their liturgical function, in Chapter 5, and the theological interpretation of the Psalter, in Chapter 6. Moreover, as we have already noted, the technical subject of reception history awaits its first publications; clearly this is not the place to pre-empt such work, though it is at least worth noting that there already exists a considerable body of modern editions of classical Christian and Jewish commentaries (a select list is provided at the end of this chapter). No doubt most of these are more appropriate to expert study, but they remind us at least that there is a long history in the discipline. And we have also already noted the work of R.E. Prothero, *The Psalms in Human Life*, which ran to four editions between 1903 and 1914. Prothero's book, if perhaps a little pious for modern taste, covers a remarkable range, and is still a unique source of evidence for the influence of the Psalms in human experience. I am tempted to suggest that there might be a market for a republication of Prothero's book.

Perhaps the most noteworthy discussion in recent years of the history of Psalms use is Holladay's survey of 'three thousand years' of the Psalms (1993). While we might, pedantically, suggest that two thousand, or two thousand five hundred years would be a more accurate figure, the practical value of what he has done is undeniable.

This is, at present, one of the most thoroughgoing studies of this subject available, though two caveats ought to be entered: first, Holladay takes a rather uncritical view of the historical setting and development of the Psalms, accepting as unproblematic the division into 'David's' psalms, 'Northern' psalms, and psalms for 'Solomon's Temple' and for the 'Second Temple'; and second, his work reflects the pious use of the Psalms by those for whom they represent a living tradition. This is perhaps best exemplified by his opening and closing chapters, in which he muses on the significance of Psalm 23.

His chapters 6, 7 and 8 provide a review of the collection and translation of the Psalms, the significance of the Dead Sea Scrolls, and the way the Psalms are used in the New Testament. These are useful enough surveys for those who might find Wilson (1985) and Flint (1997) somewhat daunting; though once again the tendency is towards a more traditional approach. For the Psalms in the New Testament, by far the most comprehensive study available is that edited by Steve Moyise and Maarten Menken (2004), in which a range of scholars cover the various books of the New Testament, together with the Dead Sea Scrolls. This work is in detail perhaps more pertinent to New Testament scholarship; nevertheless it provides a detailed resource which has – as far as I can tell – not allowed even the slightest allusion to the Psalter to escape attention!

The remainder of Holladay's Part II (chapters 9 to 14) affords a historical overview in which liturgical usage and the commentary tradition in both Judaism and Christianity up to the Renaissance are discussed (chapters 9 and 10), followed by chapters on the Reformation, the post-Tridentine Catholic Church, the nineteenth century and contemporary church use. The growth of the metrical psalm tradition is described (pp. 198–212; see further Chapter 4 in the present volume), together with a wide range of issues such as translation, further liturgical use, and the place of the Psalms in daily life. Part III (chapters 15 to 19) approaches contemporary theological and ethical questions posed by and found within the Psalter; again, we will deal with some of these issues in a later chapter, when we turn to theology and the Psalms.

A more diversified approach to the reception of the Psalms is to be found in a collection edited by Harold Attridge and Margot Fassler (2003). Covering similar historical ground to Holladay, it is more careful to give both Jewish and Christian perspectives, and is arguably more scholarly in tone. It would serve as a useful companion to Holladay; and both, taken together with my own Chapter 4 on literary uses of the Psalms, provide a wide-ranging and detailed resource for those who wish to explore the Psalms as a primary inspiration for liturgy, literature and everyday life in the centuries since the formation of Judaism and Christianity.

As a footnote to the foregoing discussion, it might be appropriate to deal with one further topic: the reception of the Psalms *within* the Old Testament itself. This can be seen in two ways: in direct liturgical quotation, most obviously in 1 Chronicles, but perhaps also in 2 Samuel 22, which cites Psalm 18 almost verbatim in the context of a song of thanksgiving for David's delivery from Saul; but more interestingly, in the use of hymnic material at crucial points in various narrative sections. James Watts has written what is, to date, the definitive study of this topic (1992), by examining Hannah's Song (1 Sam. 2.1-10), the Song of the Sea (Exod. 15.1-21), the Song of Moses (Deut. 32.1-43), the Song of Deborah (Judges 5), David's Thanksgiving (2 Samuel 22), Hezekiah's Psalm (Isa. 38.9-20), Jonah's Psalm (Jon. 2.3-10), Daniel's Praise (Dan. 2.20-23) and the 'Levitical medley' in 1 Chron. 16.8-36. Without embarking on a detailed review of Watts's conclusions, it is noteworthy that this phenomenon appears to be a genuine reception event in which, as Watts says, 'the use of psalms in narrative contexts is a literary device used to achieve compositional (narrative) goals' (1992: 186). Clearly this presupposes the existence of a genre of poetry familiar to the reader of the time, and used for a quite specific literary purpose. Watts concludes that

> one convention of Hebrew narrative genres is the inclusion of a distinguishable group of texts, consisting of psalms and a few other poems in narrative contexts of the Hebrew Bible, which through their positions and thematic commentaries contribute to narrative development. They rarely affect plot, but instead structure large blocks of material thematically, deepen the theocentric orientation of books and internal characterization of individuals, and actualize the narratives by eliciting reader participation in the songs. (1992: 197)

The implication of this thesis is, of course, that the Psalms (in some form) were a significant body of familiar material at the time when the process of expansion of narratives by means of hymns was undertaken. This seems unlikely to have been before the post-exilic restoration; something which is of importance for the dating of these narratives in their final form, and also for any discussion of the possible antiquity of materials thus embedded.

Modern editions of classical Christian and Jewish commentaries

Augustine of Hippo, Saint.
  1960–61   *St Augustine on the Psalms* (trans. Scholastica Hebgin and Felicitas Corrigan; 2 vols; London: Longmans, Green).

Braude, William G. (trans.).
  1960   *The Midrash on Psalms* (2 vols; New Haven: Yale University Press).

Calvin, J.
  1845–49   *Commentary on the Book of Psalms* (trans. James Anderson; 5 vols; Edinburgh: Calvin Translation Society).

Gross-Diaz, Theresa.
  1996   *The Psalms Commentary of Gilbert of Poitiers: From Lectio Divina to the Lecture Room* (Leiden: Brill).

Gruber, Mayer.
  1998   *Rashi's Commentary on Psalms 1–89* (Atlanta: Scholars Press).
  2004   *Rashi's Commentary on Psalms 90–150* (Leiden: Brill).

Ladouceur, David J.
  2005   *The Latin Psalter: introduction, selected text and commentary* (Bristol: Bristol Classical Press).

Theodoretus, Bishop of Cyrrhus.
  2000   *Theodoret of Cyrus Commentary on the Psalms* (trans. Robert C. Hill; 2 vols; Washington, DC: Catholic University of America Press).

Chapter 4

The Psalms as Literature

As compared with the narrative sections of scripture, the Psalms pose a more daunting challenge to literary readings for modern readers. For while narrative lends itself to visual and cinematic interpretations, and provides story lines and ironic play in abundance, the poetic themes and tropes of the Psalter and the linguistic devices it deploys are far harder to render accessible to a modern ear, even for those still familiar with it through its presence in Christian worship. And, as is the case with all poetic forms, the question of translation intrudes much more forcefully than for literature with a more directly semantic intention. Thus, though the prophetic and wisdom books are also composed broadly speaking using the *conventions* of poetry, the translator/interpreter has more to pin his or her hopes to than the poem itself. For I take it to be axiomatic that it is the very sounds and patterns, structures and phonetic interplay, which carry the soul of poetry, and without which the meaning is a decidedly poor second cousin. Of course, in a volume such as the present one, the given language is English and our concern is with the Psalms in English. But that does not entirely dispose of the problem. The choice of which biblical translation – or translations – to read from remains, and can make a significant difference. Thus it is important to say something about how this particular aspect of the literariness of the Psalms has been handled in recent decades.

In the course of this chapter I shall deal briefly with the following topics:

1 Translating the Psalms
2 Poetic features of the Psalms
3 Literary psalms: the sixteenth to nineteenth centuries
4 Literary approaches to the Psalms: the twentieth century.

As part of my discussion in section 4 I shall examine the way that psalms have been given a new lease on life through the attempt to compose genuinely modern 'interpretations' (rather than translations) of existing psalms. And although the main focus must be upon English literature, it is important here to acknowledge the use of biblical allusions and themes in the work of modern Israeli poets, who could well be said to be continuing a tradition begun nearly three millennia ago.

1. Translating the Psalms

I shall confine my remarks in this section to questions relating specifically to the rendering of the Psalms in 'suitable' English – a subset of problems relating to translation in general and the translation of poetry in particular. In my own recent study of the Psalms (Hunter 1999: 3–32) I devote two chapters to, respectively, theory of translation and the choice of a 'best fit' English version from those generally available. While it is clearly an option for each interpreter to produce his or her own 'englishing' of whichever psalms they might wish to discuss, the problem here is that the general reader is doubly excluded from the original; first, in not having direct access to Hebrew, and second, in being confronted with an opinion which may well be idiosyncratic, and about which no consensus (in the form of commentary and/or public liturgical use) has developed. Obviously this particular rubric – the requirement for a publicly acknowledged set of translations – carries far less weight where the Psalms, either as a whole or any subset of them – constitute literary pieces in English in their own right, quite regardless of their faithfulness to the originals.

In this regard, a literary collection like that produced by Donald Davie (1996) has striking virtues. It assumes (without reprinting them) the familiar Authorized versions, but provides a wide range of poems produced over some four centuries, from Coverdale to modern translators like David Frost and Gordon Jackson, which fall somewhere between my demand for public accountability on the one hand, and the freedom of the individual to interpret entirely creatively on the other. Davie makes the interesting point that up to the end of the eighteenth century it was common to find major poets trying their hand at rendering the Psalms, but that after Robert Burns 'the task is delegated to worthy persons who make few or no pretensions to being poets in (as we oddly say) their own right' (Davie 1996: xxii). He attributes this to the principles of self-expression, individualism and originality espoused by the Romantic Movement. Thus even that most overtly religious of poets, Gerard Manley Hopkins, offers nothing in the line of Psalms translation. He has one interesting piece, 'Thee, God, I come from, to thee go, / All day long I like fountain flow' (Mackenzie 1990: Poem 161), which has clear echoes of those psalms in which the poet, conscious of his/her sinfulness, seeks to hide from God, only to be discovered by God's mercy. It begins with the thought, frequently expressed in the Old Testament, that we come from and return to God. Davie understands 'Thou art indeed just, Lord' as based on Ps. 119.137-60; the superscription, however, refers rather to Jer. 12.1 (Davie 1996: 290; Mackenzie 1990: Poem 177). It is more than a little interesting, therefore, to note the number of volumes which have appeared in recent years, beginning with Peter Levi's translation in 1976, comprising either new translations of part or all of the Psalter, or compendia of translations – such as Davie, which, curiously, uses none of Levi's translations and makes no reference to that edition.

It is not possible in the short space of this chapter to pursue the detail of the arguments which rage in the battleground of translation theory; the reader is directed both to my own work already cited, and especially to Davie (1996: xxviii–lviii) where much that is sensible and insightful is offered. Davie is, admittedly, neither an Old Testament nor a Hebrew scholar, and some of what he has to say is coloured by somewhat outdated academic information. But he was a poet, and as such could offer insights which leave the more prosaic world of the scholar some distance behind. He is also, it must be said, opinionated – no bad thing when so much of what is offered as interpretation in the biblical field is anodyne. The essence of the argument – leaving aside the sheer difficulty of translating poetry – focuses on the unresolved tension between, on the one hand, the desire to match the linguistic peculiarities of the original as closely as possible and, on the other, the feeling that we should be free to represent the *sense* of the original even if that necessitates very paraphrastic translations. If the poetry of the source text is somehow to be conveyed, it seems obvious that some kind of faithfulness to the sounds and forms of the Hebrew is in order; but there are very narrow limits to what is possible. At the other extreme, we find compositions in English which could be said to be inspired by (or instigated, or prompted by) the Hebrew psalm, but which should be judged strictly in their own terms. In modest disagreement with Davie, I would include the Countess of Pembroke's magnificent version of Psalm 139 (1996: 77) in this category, as also his own adaptation of Psalm 39 (1996: 329).

The most useful modern editions are, first, five single-authored collections or part-collections: Levi (already cited), Frost *et al.* (1977), Jackson (1997), Slavitt (1996) and Wieder (2003); and second, two eclectic editions: Davie (already cited) and an earlier collection made by Wieder (1995). These last two overlap, not surprisingly, in their selections from older poets, but have almost nothing in common amongst poets of the twentieth century, and are surprisingly distinctive in their coverage of the earlier centuries (only fifteen poets are found in both anthologies, and only nineteen individual psalms are shared). The reader who wants to gain an overview of the Psalms in English since the beginning of the sixteenth century will find, both in the selections offered and in their informative introductions, much to ponder in Davies and Wieder.

2. Poetic features of the Psalms

It is questionable whether compositions designed for liturgical use should be admitted as poetry. The near-parodic admiration for Cranmer's Book of Common Prayer in self-styled literary circles (and the associated opprobrium attached to the *Alternative Service Book*) suggest that the element of distance may lend enchantment here, as in so many areas. The problem lies in the apparent discovery that *what* is said does not merit the poetic intensity of *how* it is said: for unless modern versions are hopelessly incompetent – and this is not my own experience of the matter – the difference lies in the removal of what may be a spurious element of mystery. It is manifestly not true that current English is incapable of expressing the numinous, the transcendent, or the inspirational; but it may be that traditional religious sources of these phenomena no longer carry such weight for most modern readers. It is, of course, a moot point, as we have seen already, whether the Psalms – either individually or as a whole – were composed for cultic or liturgical situations. Some surely were, some may have been adapted to such use, others may have begun life as personal *cris de coeur* and may best be understood in those terms. There is a world of difference between the emotion of Psalm 23 and that of Psalm 119: the former can still, it seems, be captured by modern readers, the latter is remote from our secular perceptions. On the other hand, a rabbinic consciousness, for which Halakhah is a primary desideratum, might warm to its elaborate and highly structured celebration of the Torah of Moses.

So far so good; but emotional response is only one small aspect of how we read poetry. A second very important dimension is that of metaphor and metonym: the standard devices by means of which language in general, and poetry in particular, attempts to create effect and enhance meaning by tempting the reader into strictly non-logical responses. This is not the place for an elementary lesson in linguistic tropes; but without some awareness of them we are likely to find ourselves adrift from the *modus operandi* of the Psalms. This is a real danger in certain religious circles, where images and phrases in the Psalms are interpreted as literal prophecies of events in (most commonly) the life of Jesus. This misreading begins in the New Testament, where Ps. 2.7 'You are my son; today I have begotten you' is cited in Mt. 3.17 to prove that Jesus is the son of God. There are numerous other examples which have successfully pre-empted the use of the Psalms for many Christians, and have led some forms of scholarly approach into a vain quest for historical contexts or social life-settings based on fragmentary evidence within the texts.

Literary tropes, even when we recognize their presence, can still present snares for the unwary. Some we do not have the linguistic ability to recognize because our knowledge of Hebrew is lacking. A good example is to be found in Ps. 29.2 which the Authorized Version renders 'Worship the Lord in *the beauty of holiness*' [my emphasis]. Later versions try 'holy splendour' (NRSV), 'the splendour of his holiness' (NIV) and 'in holy attire' (REB). What any of these phrases signifies is, sadly, a continuing mystery. Others suffer from the fact that accurate translation misrepresents the metaphor. In Hebrew the word for heart (*leb*) is regularly applied to matters of the will, the mind and the intellect; its literal translation produces a completely different English metaphor, to do with the emotions or the affections. Thus a passage like Prov. 3.5, 'Trust in the Lord with all your heart', while perfectly comprehensible in English, constitutes a religious imperative which, however valid, seems not to belong to the Hebrew original where the emphasis was closer to that of intellectual assent. Yet again, certain kinds of literary device which maintain their semantic fields through translation may nevertheless lose some of their effect through the transformation of the terms between the two cultures. 'The Lord is my shepherd' undoubtedly depends upon a profession which belongs to both ancient Israel and modern society; but that may be all they have in common. I do not imagine that the psalmist conceived of him/herself as being coralled by a couple of sheepdogs, for example. Another pervasive example, the frequent use made of kingship and autocratic hereditary rule to describe God and God's relationships with humankind, poses problems of a different kind for peoples familiar with democracy and constitutional monarchy or elected presidential office. The only models we have currently for autocracy are negative in the extreme. These examples, and many others, present problems for translation on the one hand and for our reception of the Psalms' poetic aspects on the other. A recent study – Brown (2002) – addresses the question of metaphors directly, though mostly in the interests of explaining how they function theologically and in their contextual terms. Some of Gordon Jackson's compositions address the contemporary problems head-on in attempting to provide meaningful renderings. Here is one example which might serve as a taster for others in his collection:

Psalm 2
Why are the nations up in arms, and men drawn into insane dreams?
The world's rulers are in accord – against God and the Lord's Anointed:
'Old God's authority is at an end – long live the Revolution!'
The Lord in heaven is laughing; to him their threats are a joke.
But one day his top will blow, and his fury flow like lava.
Here on my holy mountain, behold the man, the Anointed
I say what I hear the Lord speak –
    You are my Son; this day I have begotten you:
The nations are yours for the asking, the ends of the earth your estate:
With a sceptre of iron judge them; smash them to smithereens.
Learn wisdom smartly, O Captains and Rulers, remember your place:
Bow to the Lord in fear, and rejoice in him with trembling:
Kiss the Son, stay his displeasure, and beware his infolded fire;
Once it erupts it will engulf all but the blessed he shelters.
(Jackson 1997: 13)

There is a neat juxtaposition of current usage with eschatological threat in this translation which almost succeeds in injecting new force into the somewhat tired imagery of empires at war that inhabits the original, while the emphasized passages have the effect of removing the troublesome Christological reading from direct to reported speech ('I say what I hear the Lord speak') which restores its metaphoric character and strips out its spurious theological authority.

The Psalms are also replete with structural devices which present varying degrees of difficulty. The phenomenon of parallelism, first given prominence in modern scholarship by Lowth (1787 [1847]: 208–21), can to some extent survive translation – though where it depends crucially on the order of words in the original it is often masked. Here translators may have the choice which poetic convention offers of unusual word order in English, but surprisingly few take it up. There is a pleasing instance in Ps. 121.3-5 (to which

we have already had occasion to make reference, in Chapter 1), where
the Hebrew order is:

> v. 3   He will not let your foot slip,
>   He will not slumber,
>   *He who protects you.*
> v. 4   For sure, he will not slumber,
>   He will not fall asleep,
>   *He who protects Israel.*
> v. 5   *Yahweh is your protector*

Notice the skill with which the psalm delays the subject, at the same
time as it enhances the identity of the subject in three stages, from
the simple 'he who protects you' through the more all-embracing 'he
who protects Israel' to the final revelation that it is none other than
Yahweh who is the protector. Yet the majority of English versions
ignore this aspect of the verse. For comparison, there follow, in order,
those of the Authorized Version (which does not set out the text as
poetry), the NIV, the JPS Tanakh, and the NRSV:

> v .3   He will not suffer thy foot to be moved: he that keepeth thee will not
>   slumber.
> v. 4   Behold, he that keepeth Israel shall neither slumber nor sleep.
> v. 5   The Lord is thy keeper.

> v. 3   He will not let your foot slip,
>   he who watches over you will not slumber;
> v. 4   indeed, he who watches over Israel
>   will neither slumber nor sleep.
> v. 5   The Lord watches over you.

> v. 3   He will not let your foot give way;
>   your guardian will not slumber;
> v. 4   See, the guardian of Israel
>   neither slumbers nor sleeps!
> v. 5   The Lord is your guardian

> v. 3   He will not let your foot be moved;
>   he who keeps you will not slumber.
> v. 4   He who keeps Israel
>   will neither slumber nor sleep.
> v. 5   The Lord is your keeper;

These versions all lose the Hebrew poetic effect by reordering each of verses 3 and 4; yet it poses no serious problems of translation, as my own basic translation (above) shows.

This failure to follow what is a rather central aspect of the structure of the Psalms is interesting, for it suggests that the primary motivation for most scholarly translation was to reach a quite conventional kind of received English. Many of the secondary versions to be found in Davie and Wieder will have based themselves on earlier English renditions, though Levi's translation of Psalm 121 directly from the Hebrew is no better. Berlin (1985) and Kugel (1981) are still the best studies of parallelism in the Psalms, though somewhat dependent on a knowledge of Hebrew. Kugel's book has the added advantage of containing a 'history of ideas about parallelism – and biblical poetry generally – from antiquity to the present' (1981: vii). It serves as a salutary reminder that even Lowth was not the originator of the study of parallelism, but rather the transmitter into modern discourse of a phenomenon already remarked upon in rabbinic discourse. In my own book I examine structure, including parallelism, more generally (Hunter 1999: 46–61). It is of course difficult to go more than a certain distance into structural features on the basis of translations alone; and this is even more true of aspects such as paronomasia, assonance, consonance and dissonance, alliteration, and the repetition of key words and roots. But such difficulties are true of all poetry in translation, and need not delay us for long here. Those who are interested to explore the phenomenon of classical Hebrew poetry further should take up Watson (1984) for technical details and Alter (1980) or Fisch (1988) for a more literary analysis. A more user-friendly account of the technical side of Hebrew poetry is to be found in Petersen and Richards (1992). Recent studies, particularly those by Fokkelman (2001, 2002), and Terrien (2003), have drawn attention to and focused on the 'strophic form' (Terrien's term) of individual compositions. Their work, while highly technical, suggests a new avenue which may deliver some insights in the poetry of the Psalms.

I began this section by querying whether it is proper to treat the Psalms as poetry; I suggest that the evidence we have reviewed is sufficient to provide a qualified affirmative, but only if a serious effort is made to represent these works in translation with their recognizable structural features, while at the same time endeavouring to revivify the metaphoric and metonymic basis from which they operate. This is in many ways the exact reverse of what has commonly happened; but the work of Jackson and others offers some hope that surprising and refreshingly new poems can still be found in this ancient collection.

3. Literary psalms: the sixteenth to nineteenth centuries

The great period of biblical translation which culminated in the Authorized (King James) Version stimulated a parallel literary interest in the Psalms which influenced poets such as Donne, Herbert, Milton and the Sidneys. From the review of Davie and Wieder in section 1, we have already seen that they represent only a fraction of what was a very considerable activity. Between them, these two collections represent 78 different poets, of whom only about a dozen were active in the twentieth century. Given the huge influence of the Bible in literature of the pre-Romantic periods this is hardly surprising; what is more interesting is the significant recent interest in extensive translation since 1976 (Levi, Frost, Jackson, Slavitt and Wieder), which seems to suggest that the modern decline in influence of the Authorized Version has spurred efforts to recapture a body of verse which was fast disappearing from view.

Some psalms, of course, have never lost their fascination: the *De Profundis* ('Out of the depths', Psalm 130); the exiles' vengeful lament (Psalm 137) 'by the waters of Babylon' – not least for its incarnation at the hands of Boney M; the great celebration of the ineluctable presence of God which is Psalm 139 ('If I take the wings of the morning, and dwell in the uttermost parts of the sea, even there shall thy hand lead me' vv. 9f., AV); and of course Psalm 23 whose words have accompanied countless of the dead on their final journey, and which Holladay (1993) characterizes as 'an American secular icon'. Others are heard by secular audiences in a variety of choral guises: 'Why do the heathen rage' (Ps. 2.1) in the *Messiah*; 'Bringing in the sheaves' (Ps. 126.6) in the well-known Spiritual; Stravinsky's *Symphony of Psalms* (38.13-14; 39.2-4; 150); Bernstein's *Chichester Psalms* (108.2; 100; 23; 2.1-4; 131; 133.1); and the antiphonal performance of psalms in the Anglican Choral Evensong – for many today as much an aesthetic as a religious experience. Through their use in the Book of Common Prayer many individual phrases from the Psalms have entered the common stock of English; the considerable number included in *The Oxford Dictionary of Quotations* is eloquent testimony to this enduring aspect of the literary role of the Psalms.

Historically speaking, the stimulus to serious literary work on the Psalms came from the Reformation emphasis on vernacular worship and the particular need for English psalms, given their key role in the liturgy. Most of those who have direct experience of them in this respect will know them either from the uninspired and generally uninspiring metrical versions – which are occasionally redeemed by magnificent music – or from the prose translations of Miles Coverdale in the Book of Common Prayer. The challenge to create truly *poetic* translations was first, and arguably most impressively met by Sir Philip Sidney (Psalms 1–43) and his sister Mary, Countess of Pembroke (Psalms 44–150, and revisions of her brother's work). Both, of course, worked from English prose translations; but their real strength lay in the application to this work of secular poetic conventions and a willingness to be adventurous in structure, rhyme, metre and metaphor. R.E. Pritchard (1992: 8) offers this assessment:

> The 'Sidneian Psalms', as Donne called them in his celebratory poem, begun by Sir Philip Sidney in the 1580s and completed after his death by his sister Mary, constituted, in their fusion of technical sophistication and religious commitment, a major cultural intervention. This poetry, so little known nowadays, which did so much to transform the quality of seventeenth-century religious lyric – it is hard to imagine the poetry of George Herbert being the same without it – was a considered response to the writers' complex political, religious, literary and personal situation.

The truth of this assessment may be easily demonstrated by setting alongside each other for comparison Mary Sidney's rendering of the first four verses of Psalm 130 with that of Sternhold and Hopkins (1562) and the Scottish Metrical Psalter of 1560–64. The last is notably more succinct than either of the other two:

Mary Sidney
>   From depth of grief
>   Where drowned I lie,
>   Lord for relief
>   To thee I cry:
>   My earnest, vehement, crying, praying,
>   Grant quick, attentive hearing, weighing.
>   O Lord, if thou
>   Offences mark,
>   Who shall not bow
>   To bear the cark?
>   But with thy justice mercy dwelleth,
>   Whereby thy worship more excelleth.

Sternhold and Hopkins
>   Lord, unto thee I make my moan,
>   when dangers me oppress;
>   I call, I sigh, complain, and groan,

> trusting to find release
> Hearken, O Lord, to my request,
>   unto my suit incline,
> And let thine ears, O Lord, be pressed
>   to hear this prayer of mine
> O Lord our God, if thou survey
>   our sins, and them peruse,
> Who shall escape? Or who dare say,
>   I can myself excuse.
> But thou art merciful and free,
>   and boundless in thy grace,
> That we might always careful be
>   to fear before thy face.

Scottish Metrical Psalter
> Lord, from the depths to thee I cried.
>   My voice, Lord, do thou hear:
> Unto my supplications' voice
>   Give an attentive ear.
> Lord, who shall stand, if thou, O Lord,
>   Shouldst mark iniquity?
> But yet with thee forgiveness is,
>   That feared thou mayest be.

It would be unkind to berate the metrical versions for not being what they never intended to be, or to forget the exigencies of strict metre necessitated by the simple tunes required for popular worship. While it is sad that for a great many people their only knowledge of the Psalms as poetry consists of a body of what is, at best, mundane verse and, at worst, doggerel, nevertheless this body of work too is part of the literary heritage of the Psalms, and one which has shown remarkable powers both of survival and of influence. Nevertheless, without making unreasonable claims for the Sidneys, their influence is undoubted, certainly meriting Donne's accolade 'They tell us *why*, they teach us *how* to sing' (Davie 1996: 98).

While critics are agreed that George Herbert was influenced by the Sidneys' psalms, it is perhaps curious that he produced little himself by way of psalms translation. Only one is known, a metrical version of Psalm 23, which is remarkably unlike his other verse. Davie notes the conjecture that 'he contrived a special rusticity so as to appeal to an unlettered congregation used to the old version of Sternhold and Hopkins' (Davie 1996: 117). However, one scholar has suggested that, from a religious point of view, Herbert may have seen virtue in those very lame and ill-formed verses which would have been used by his congregation, and quotes a verse from 'The Elixir' in support:

> All may of thee partake:
> Nothing can be so mean,
> Which with his tincture (for thy sake)
>   Will not grow bright and clean. (Freer 1972: 12)

This poem itself has something of the structure and rhythm of the metrical psalms, though its use of these is far more subtle. It is not suprising that it has become itself a well-known hymn, together with 'Let all the world in every corner sing' and 'King of Glory, King of Peace' (which has some links with Psalm 116). The reminiscences of the style of the Sidneys are clear in all three, and suggest that the liturgical tradition missed an opportunity when it failed to develop these as choral items. Herbert himself, arguably, writes *as if* he were a psalmist, and a number of his poems can be read in that way. Consider, for instance, 'Affliction (IV)': here is precisely the mood and pattern of so many psalms of lamentation, though in Herbert's individual voice. I quote here the first and last two stanzas, and suggest a comparison with Psalms 57 and 70 from a fairly long list of possible exemplars:

> Broken in pieces all asunder,
>   Lord hunt me not,
>   A thing forgot,
> Once a poore creature, now a wonder,
>   A wonder tortur'd in the space
>   Betwixt this world and that of grace.
> Oh help, my God! let not their plot,
>   Kill them and me,
>   And also thee,
> Who art my life: dissolve the knot,
>   As the sun scatters by his light
>   All the rebellions of the night.
> Then shall those powers, which work for grief,
>   Enter thy pay,
>   And day by day
> Labour thy praise, and my relief;
>   With care and courage building me,
>   'Till I reach heav'n, and much more thee. (Patrides: 1974: 105)

These, and similar examples, testify to the truth of Patrides' claim that 'so profoundly was Herbert engaged with the Psalter that its echoes reverberate across his poetry, to an extent unmatched by any other poet in English Literature' (1974: 10).

Herbert succeeds in conveying a religious sensibility which, however foreign to the modern consciousness, is given eloquent voice by poetry which combines elegance of structure with a genuine passion. His older contemporary, Donne, while notable for his celebratory poem on the Sidney Psalms, affords surprisingly little else of direct relevance to our subject. His specifically religious poetry ('On The Progress of the Soul', 1612, and a variety of groups including the 'Holy Sonnets', the 'Divine Meditations', and a 'Litany', written probably at various points through his career) is too precisely focused on Christian themes to offer any direct echo of the Psalms – this is especially true of the 'Holy Sonnets'. The 'Divine Meditations', a sequence of nineteen sonnets, is infused in its earlier stanzas with something of the psalmists' sense of being both creaturely and unhappy – made by God, but despairing in the face of death and the enemies of the soul. But Donne's theology is in the end too Calvinist to be truly in harmony with the thought of the psalmists, who never – even in their bleakest moments – abandoned the hope that the individual might experience God's mercy. Compare, for example, the concluding lines of the 'Divine Meditations' with the sentiments of the psalm whose superscription attributes it to David after Nathan takes him to task for the Bathsheba affair:

> I durst not view heaven yesterday; and today
> In prayers and flattering speeches I court God:
> Tomorrow I quake with true fear of his rod.
> So my devout fits come and go away
> Like a fantastic ague: save that here
> Those are my best days, when I shake with fear.

> (Smith 1976: 309–17 (317))

Psalm 51.7-13
> Purge me with hyssop, and I shall be clean;
>   wash me, and I shall be whiter than snow.
> Let me hear joy and gladness;
>   let the bones that you have crushed rejoice.
> Hide your face from my sins,
>   and blot out all my iniquities.
> Create in me a clean heart, O God,
>   and put a new and right spirit within me.

> Do not cast me away from your presence,
>   and do not take your holy spirit from me.
> Restore to me the joy of your salvation,
>   and sustain in me a willing spirit.
> Then will I teach transgressors your ways,
>   and sinners will return to you.

The psychological difference is instructive. Donne, who never committed any crime as heinous as murder in the interest of adultery, finds it hard to conceive of mercy, while the psalmist's verse is imbued with optimism, however sombre his crimes.

Donne has one significant work of biblical translation – a version of Lamentations entitled 'The Lamentations of Jeremy' (Smith 1976: 334–46) – in a rigorous ten-syllable metre with a strict *aabb* rhyming pattern over virtually all of its 390 lines. The character of the biblical book of Lamentations is that of an extended psalm of lament, but of a national rather than individual kind. This might therefore be seen as Donne's contribution to the genre of Psalms translation; as such, it perhaps suits a certain melancholic note to his own character, and is in keeping with – though superior to – the techniques of the metrical Psalms. Thus, summing up this aspect of Donne and Herbert, we find in the former a clear respect for the psalms of Philip and Mary Sidney, with little sign of emulation; and in the latter an undoubted stylistic influence through his religious poetry in general, but ironically only one psalm rendered, and that in the standard metrical mode. While this may reflect simple preference on the part of these poets, it is tempting to speculate that something in the liturgical use of the Psalms themselves precluded a genuinely literary approach; the Sidneys constitute a potential that was never truly developed – until, dare we suggest, the twentieth century.

Milton produced versions of Psalms 1–8 (composed in 1653) and 81–88 (composed in 1648), together with a versification of Psalm 136 which is familiar as the hymn 'Let us with a gladsome mind', supposedly composed when he was fifteen, and a paraphrase of Psalm 114 from the same period. The difference between the two groups is striking: the earlier group is in strict common metre (8/6/8/6) rhymed *abab*, as if they were deliberately modelled upon the metrical collections. Despite their qualities, they did not become part of that liturgical tradition, leaving Milton's main contribution to worship the somewhat awkward piece from his teenage years. The second group to be composed is poetically more interesting in its deployment of a variety of metre, rhythm and rhyme pattern. Psalm 3 in particular uses one of the forms found in the Sidney Psalms, and the sheer diversity that is compressed into this short collection is reminiscent of the same phenomenon in Sidney. A brief quotation from Psalm 3 must suffice to illustrate this point:

> Lord how many are my foes
>> How many are those
>>> That in arms against me rise;
>>>> Many are they
> That of my life distrustfully thus say,
> No help for him in God there lies.
> But thou Lord art my shield, my glory,
>> Thee through my story
>>> Th' exalter of my head I count;
>>>> Aloud I cry'd
> Unto Jehovah, he full soon reply'd
> And heard me from his holy mount. (cited in Radzinowicz 1989: 93)

Milton, interestingly, does seem to have worked directly from the Hebrew, a fact which, according to Mary Ann Radzinowicz, may have contributed to the metrical freedom he displays in these translations:

> Milton's willingness to translate eight Psalms in a wide variety of metres without imposing a traditional English one suggests that he thought Hebrew verse observed its own kind of ancient freedom, overruling the preference for any single English metrical practice. Like the verse of Pindar, that of David privileged rhythm over meter. (1989: 94)

This obviously fails to account for the strict metre and rhyme in Psalms 81–88. Did Milton work from English exemplars in this instance, or are we to read them as a virtuoso performance in a strict form which, having been accomplished, left him free to experiment in Psalms 1–8? Whatever the answer to these questions, we find in Milton's versions a virtual synopsis of the English Psalms tradition of the sixteenth and seventeenth centuries.

Three other names merit mention: Isaac Watts and Christopher Smart in the eighteenth century, and James Montgomery in the nineteenth. Watts might best be described as a jobbing versifier, while Montgomery is more broadly a hymnographer, whose work has contributed hugely (as indeed has Watts's) to hymnaries in most anglophone Christian traditions. Smart is more interesting – an erratic poet most famous for his long unfinished poem 'Jubilate Agno' in which (among many other things) he celebrates his cat

Jeoffry. The poem was written during a period of incarceration for supposed insanity – though one might imagine that a man who could find reason to praise God through his pet cat was saner than most of us. Both Davie and Wieder include generous examples of Smart's versions; Wieder provides seventeen: only Mary Sidney has a greater number in *The Poets' Book of Psalms*. A flavour of his work is to be found in Psalm 134, which conforms to a kind of faintly jolly metrical rhythm, but succeeds nonetheless in conveying a certain strangeness not out of keeping with the poet and his source:

> Attend to the musick divine
>> Ye people of God with the priest,
> At once your Hosanna combine
>> As meekly ye bow to the east.
> Ye servants that look to the lights
>> Which blaze in the house of the Lord,
> And keep up the watch of the nights
>> To bless each apartment and ward,
> The holy of holies review,
>> And lift up your hands with your voice,
> And there sing your anthem anew,
>> In praise to Jehova rejoice.
> The Lord that made heav'n and earth
>> Which rules o'er the night and the day,
> His blessing bestow on your mirth,
>> And hear you whenever ye pray. (Davie 1996: 251)

4. Literary approaches to the Psalms: the twentieth century

A path which I have not chosen to go down in this chapter is to review the many biblical translations which have appeared in English since the nineteenth century. It would be futile here either to list or to attempt to evaluate what is a burgeoning literary, religious and (it must be said) commercial enterprise. Thus I will confine my comments in this final section to translations which have either a clear poetic purpose or a liturgical direction independently of biblical translation *per se*. This means that I will *not* here consider Harry Mowvley's *The Psalms: Introduced and Newly Translated for Today's Readers* (1989), but *will* note the so-called 'Gelineau Psalms' because of their explicit liturgical purpose. The principal collections, then, are the Gelineau Psalms (1963), Levi, Frost, Slavitt, Jackson and Wieder. Of these, two are expressly liturgical in purpose (Gelineau and Frost); the other four seek explicitly to make English poetry out of the Psalms. The so-called Gelineau Psalter emerged in the 1950s from the French Jerusalem Bible project, and was a deliberate attempt to render the Psalms in such a manner that they could easily be sung or recited in a fashion true to the original Hebrew poetry. The musical settings are those of Joseph Gelineau, the translations were made by a team of scholars bearing this context specifically in mind: 'Special attention was paid to the rhythmic structure of the poetry of the psalms, and this allowed a sung or recited psalmody to be fashioned on the basis of the analogy that exists between the Hebrew tonic rhythm and that of our modern languages' (Gelineau 1963: 10). Similarly, the preface to the edition under the name of David Frost (who in fact took the work of a panel of Hebrew scholars and 'prepared a rendering in an English style and rhythm suitable for singing or reading aloud in church' (1977: 14)) makes it clear that the needs of singing, chanting and recitation as part of the liturgy were an essential part of the process.

Turning to the four literary translations, I have reproduced below for purposes of comparison the translations of Psalm 100 made by them, since they may be assumed to have an explicitly poetic purpose. I have arranged them in pairs, the first two being by English poets (Levi and Jackson), the second pair North American (Wieder and Slavitt). They illustrate rather effectively the different options open to those bold enough to undertake such an enterprise, and do so along what appear to be cultural lines (though admittedly the sample is far too small to permit of any sweeping conclusions). Thus Levi, certainly, and Jackson to a degree preserve a kind of sobriety of tone, a more literal faithfulness to the original which mutes their own poetic voice. The other two quite strikingly depart from the Hebrew to create new poems which have their own very clear authorial sound, without losing a recognizable connection with the Hebrew. The reader is invited to make his or her own appraisal of the results.

Peter Levi

Shout to God all the earth,
serve God with rejoicing,
come to him with shouting and gladness.
Know that God is God,
he made us, we are his,
his people and the sheep of his flock.
Enter his gates with thanksgiving
and his courts with praise.
Give thanks to him and bless his name.

God is good and his mercy is everlasting,
and his faithfulness is for every generation.

Gordon Jackson

Give glory to God, all men of the earth,
    be glad that you serve him,
        let his presence fill your hearts to bursting
           and his goodness fill your praises;
You know that the Lord is God,
    that he it was made us,
      that we are his,
        his very own flock that he loves and provides for;
So enter with confidence through his gates,
    fill his courts with your praises,
      give him such thanks as you have to give him,
        and bless his holy name;
For the Lord is good and his love will never run out,
    and his truth will stand the test of all generations.

Laurance Wieder

It helps to make a lot of noise
When on earth. We did not,
Were modest, too, until God made us
Enter squally bawling thank-yous
In our lifetime, children's children.

David Slavitt

Let every nation chorale to the Lord
a Dio, con brio
    in love and joy before Him.
    Sing to him and adore Him
      with a resonant tonic chord,
        acknowledging God as the Lord.
He made us and all else there is.
We are his sheep; our meadow is His.
    In joy we intone our thanks and praise.
    let us in elegant harmony raise
      our voices to sing;
      He is good, and He is one,
      from mother to daughter, from father to son.

I turn finally to a brief comment on the theory of literary approaches to the Psalms. There is, of course, considerable overlap

with theory in general, for which there is ample resource in other
places. My own book provides an overview which those who wish to
test the postmodern waters may find helpful (Hunter 1999: 62–99);
however, it must be said that there is not a wealth of material on
this subject, though there are many studies of individual psalms and
groups of psalms. More often than not they deal with historical-
critical and linguistic points which belong to a different field of
specialism. Robert Alter's *Art of Biblical Poetry* (1980) is a notable
exception: well worth reading both for its wealth of information and
for its elegant style. Detailed discussion of a whole range of literary
aspects of biblical poetry is provided, taking in wisdom and prophetic
texts as well as the Psalms, and concluding with a brief chapter, 'The
Life of the Tradition' which addresses some of the topics we have
considered at more length in this essay. Alter concludes his study with
a brief discussion of a modern Israeli poem (by Tuvia Rüvner) which
opens with a double citation from the Psalms (Alter 1990: 211–13).
Virtually all of the language in the poem is recognizably biblical, yet
also recognizably modern Hebrew in its original form. It is certainly
the case that there is considerable intertextuality in the biblical
Psalms; thus the contemporary poet's use of biblical material to
create modern poetry (which is highly developed in Israeli verse) has
close analogies with the Psalms themselves. For even though modern
poems rarely serve a *directly* religious purpose, the very denseness of
biblical allusion creates an expectation and a response in the reader
which is not that distant from what one might experience reading a
biblical psalm and recognizing its intertext: a good example is the way
that Psalm 8 toys with the creation account in Genesis 1 and 2. The
recognition of this link allows the reader space to read between, and
indeed outside, the lines and thereby to build a response in a far wider
interpretive field than he or she might at first have expected. While
modern Israeli poetry is technically outside the remit of this essay,
it is perhaps worth noting that the poem by Tuvia is by no means
an isolated example; the traditions of the Psalter (and of the Old
Testament as a whole) are to be found alive and well in Israel today.
Perhaps the most stimulating study in English of this phenomenon
is David Jacobson's *Does David Still Play Before You?* (1996); for
a complete review of Hebrew verse through three millennia, Carmi
(1981) is indispensable. Finally, two individual studies deserve
mention: Ruth Kartun-Blum's *Profane Scriptures* (1999), which has
many interesting things to say about the continuing role of biblical
motifs, language, and traditions in contemporary Israeli poetry
– including a long and fascinating chapter on transformations of the
Aqedah (the Binding of Isaac); and Yair Mazor's study of the poetry

of Asher Reich which draws out his use of Mishnaic, Talmudic and biblical references (2003).

I shall conclude with a brief account of an important essay by Harold Fisch, 'Psalms: The Limits of Subjectivity' (Fisch 1988: 104–35). In it he asks whether, unlike other biblical poetry which often has a strong dialogic character, the Psalms can be read as meditations in the Romantic sense of 'a self-consciousness which expresses itself essentially in monologue' (1988: 108). He goes on to argue that rather than monologues the Psalms are a kind of 'whispered inner dialogue', but one in which, because of the communal dimension, the 'I/thou' regularly segues into a 'we/thou' (1988: 108–14). But a further reversal takes place, as

> the trials and struggles of the community often take on the character of a lonely, individual ordeal in which the suffering soul cries out to God and is answered. What one would want to say is that, paradoxically, the ongoing covenant drama involving God and the people is constantly interiorized to become the drama of a lonely soul, crying in anguish, trusting and despairing. The people in short take on the marks of a lyrical subjectivity, giving us idiolect and sociolect all together. (1988: 105)

The Psalms are also characterized by a level of formulaic language – words conscious of themselves and of their contexts. 'Every phrase in the Psalms is a kind of quotation; ... To put it very simply, we could say that we have here a kind of poetry reflexively conscious of the importance of poetry' (1988: 119). A fitting observation with which to conclude this chapter.

Chapter 5

Liturgical Approaches

1. Introduction

There are several ways in which this rather obviously important topic might be approached, and all have been used, with varying degrees of success. The starting point, undoubtedly, is to look at the festivals we find reported in the Old Testament, either in the form of prescriptions for their practice, or as historical account. Next, and to some extent overlapping with the first, we might enquire within the Psalms themselves for hints as to liturgical use, looking for instance for references to festivals or rituals, evidence of processions, signs of antiphonal use, and the presence of technical language. Third, we have the option of examining the wider context of the Old Testament to see whether material from the Psalter is used in clearly liturgical settings: if, for example, we read of a Passover celebration, is it attended by anything from the Psalter, or at least material analogous to existing psalms? Fourth, it is possible to look at the directions for surviving festivals from neighbouring cultures, and the hymnic materials they used, to see whether these offer any helpful parallels. And lastly, we can look at Jewish and Christian sources of the first centuries CE in case there are any signs of continuity of use. Here, for example, both the Mishnah and the New Testament are essential witnesses, together with the Dead Sea Scrolls. We have looked at the last of these in a previous chapter, and so in the present chapter I will confine myself to the first two.

2. Israel's festivals

But first I want to consider an even more basic perspective: a review of the festivals themselves as they are reported in the Old Testament.

Surely, if the Psalms were composed for Israel's liturgical seasons, we will find some correspondence between the principal feasts on the one hand and key aspects of the Psalms on the other? However, it is somewhat surprising to discover that the festivals themselves, apart from the three rather fixed points in the calendar when they take place, are by no means the subject of clarity or harmony. The following tables set out the references to the five principal named festivals, and also indicate those places where the formula 'three times a year' is recorded. The fixed times are (in rough equivalents of the standard western calendar): mid-March (14th Nisan), early to mid-May (7th Sivan), and mid-September (Tishri). These vary, of course, since the Jewish year is of a different length, based on lunar phases, and uses an additional month every now and again to restore the conformity with the solar year.

Table 5.1

Torah

Exod. 12.1–13.10 [M, P]; Exod.23.14-17 [M, 3x]; Exod. 34.18-25 [M, P, Sh, 3x]; Lev. 16 [Y]; Lev. 23 [M, P, Sh, Y, S]; Num. 28.16–29.40 [M, P, Sh, Y, S]; Deut. 16.1-17 [M, P, Sh, S, 3x]; Deut. 31.10 [S].

Historical & Prophetic Books

Josh. 5.10-12 [M, P]; 2 Kgs 23.21-23 [P]; Ezek. 45.17-25 [M, P]; Zech. 14.16-19 [S].

Writings

Ezra 3.4 [S]; Ezra 6.19-22 [M, P]; Neh. 8.13-18 [S]; 2 Chron. 8.13 [M, Sh, S, 3x]; 2 Chron. 30.1-27 [M, P]; 2 Chron. 35.1-19 [M, P].

Note: M = Matsot (Unleavened Bread); P = Pesah (Passover); Sh = Shevuot (Weeks); S = Sukkot (Booths); Y = Yom Kippur (Atonement); 3x = three times a year

Table 5.2

	matsot	pesah	shevuot	yom kippur	sukkot	3×
Exod. 23.14-17	●					●
Exod. 34.18-25	●	●	●			●
Deut. 16.1-17	●	●	●		●	●
2 Chron. 8.13	●		●		●	●
Lev. 16				●		
Lev. 23	●	●	●	●	●	
Num. 28.16–29.40	●	●	●	●	●	
Exod. 12.1–13.10	●	●				
Deut. 31.10					●	
Ezek. 45.17-25	●	●				
Zech. 14.16-19					●	
Josh. 5.10-12	●	●				
2 Kgs 23.21-23		●				
Ezra 3.4					●	
Ezra 6.19-22	●	●				
Neh. 8.13-18					●	
2 Chron. 30.1-27	●	●				
2 Chron. 35.1-19	●	●				

Note: Table 5.1 sets out the data in the order of the books of the Old Testament according to the Jewish tradition. Table 5.2 provides the same information grouped to show (1) those passages which refer explicitly to three times in the year; (2) those which refer to Yom Kippur; (3) other theoretical rubrics; and (4) records of actual performances of festivals. It could be argued that Exodus 12–13 should belong to the fourth group rather than the third, since it describes the first 'historical' passover.

Several observations are in order. First, Yom Kippur, or the Day of Atonement, is a special case. It only appears in Levitians 16 and 23, and Numbers 29, both regarded as rather late sections of Torah; whether it should be regarded as having been one of the 'three' festivals is doubtful. Second, though there are three *times* in the year for festival, there were evidently more than three festivals (even when we disregard Hanukkah and Purim, which only emerged in the late post-exilic period). In the tables five are noted, a fact that may imply some diversity of tradition or merging of separate events. In addition, in Exod. 23 and 34 the number three includes simple agricultural designations like 'harvest', 'first fruits', and 'ingathering at the end of the year' (Exod. 23.16-17), and 'first fruits', 'wheat harvest', and 'ingathering at the turn of the year' (Exod. 34.22). Thus we should perhaps extend the list to at least seven, by including 'first fruits' and 'ingathering'.

It might be possible to rationalize this complex situation as follows: the earliest stage was represented by nature festivals, speculatively relating to firstborn lambs in spring (hence the passover ritual sacrifice), then first fruits in May or June (note the historicized context for this in the 'Wandering Aramaean' liturgy of Deut. 26.1-11), and finally the 'ingathering' at the autumnal end of the year. A second stage might be identified in the combining of an essentially naturalistic feast (Unleavened Bread) with that of Passover, which must have from early times been associated with the origin legends of Israel. That this might have some claim to be the first of the festivals to be formalized in a specifically Israelite cult can be seen, perhaps, in the priority given to this point in the calendar in Exodus 12–13; 23; and 34, and further in the fact that Passover by far predominates in the records of actual festival observances. It must be noted, however, that the absence of any reference to Passover in 2 Chron. 8.12-13 is difficult to explain:

> Then Solomon offered up burnt-offerings to the Lord on the altar of the Lord that he had built in front of the vestibule, as the duty of each day required, offering according to the commandment of Moses for the sabbaths, the new moons, and the three annual festivals – the festival of unleavened bread, the festival of weeks, and the festival of booths.

The place of Weeks and Booths is even harder to clarify. The latter is not referred to in Exodus, but is prominent elsewhere. Along with Passover in Ezekiel, it is the only festival to be noted by name anywhere in the prophets, in Zechariah. It is also the only other festival for which there are historical accounts, and it is given a special role in Deut. 31.9-13, in the context of a Torah-renewal event. Given the natural significance of the autumnal year's end, which is important in festivals in Babylonia which are often cited as parallels, the prominence of Sukkot is not surprising. Commentators have regularly identified its traces in psalms which celebrate the harvest.

There are, in fact, only two places where a named festival appropriate to each point in the calendar is listed together with the 'three times a year' formula. One is 2 Chron. 8.12-13, which we have already noted as being defective, and the other is Deut. 16.1-17, which now begins to look like a harmonizing summary trying to bring order to a slightly chaotic situation (rather like Tatian's *Diatessaron*, the earliest extant attempt to harmonize the Gospels). But then, as if there was not sufficient ambiguity already, along comes Yom Kippur, the johnny-come-lately, sneaking in under the cover of the Torah, but surely a post-exilic development with no real roots in the kind of annual pattern which seems to have been the mark of the pre-exilic cult.

What are the implications for our liturgical interpretation of the Psalter of this complex and somewhat indeterminate situation? I think that we can expect to find some echoes of the traditions of the Passover – and there are certainly psalms which provide historical recitals including the events of Exodus, or which poetically or mythically recall the victory of Yahweh over the waters, or which might allude to elements of the ceremony. Pss. 68.7-23; 78.12-55; 80.8-11; 81; 99.6-7; 105.23-45; 106.7-33; 135.8-12; and 136.10-22 all provide accounts of the Egypt and wilderness traditions, and may be compared with Exod. 15.1-18. It does not seem to be unreasonable to make the obvious connection with cultic events. Poetic or mythic references to the defeat of the waters are to be found in Pss. 68.7-10, 22; 74.12-14; 77.11-20; and 114. I do not include here instances of the psalmist him/herself being rescued from the threat of drowning, such as in Ps. 18.15-19 and 124.1-5, though Jonah 2, with its explicit references to the 'reeds', does combine the two themes. Finally, and most elusively, specific references to elements of the ritual *might* be seen in two uses of the idea of the cup, one positive, in Ps. 116.13 (the cup of salvation), and one negative, in Ps. 75.8-9 (the cup of wrath). These, however, are hardly conclusive, and may only gain their significance from the later Passover ritual described in Mishnah.

The importance of the autumn festival is perhaps reflected in such psalms as 126, which uses the metaphor of the joy at harvest (vv. 5-6; compare also 107.37f.); 128, with its description of the family as a fruitful vine and olive shoots (v. 3; compare 80.8-11); or 129 where the failure of the harvest is used to describe the fate of the wicked (vv.

6-8). Other psalms which contain material which might be appropriate to harvest include 65.9-13 and 67.6-7. The processional element of Ps. 118.19-29 has often been associated with Sukkot, perhaps because of the custom of waving the *lulav* branches at that festival. However, as with the specific rituals of Passover, it is not clear when this custom first arose, and whether Psalm 118 records it or represents an accidental similarity. The wording of Lev. 23.40 provides independent support for this association; but by contrast, the 'Palm Sunday' episode in the Gospels further confuses the issue, since it cites Psalm 118 (Mt. 21.9 and parallels), and would appear therefore to relate to Passover. One further possibility may be proposed: we have seen that Deut. 31.10 makes a connection between Torah and Sukkot, in the form of a kind of covenant ceremony. If this is not merely theoretical, it may be no coincidence that Psalm 119, the great Torah psalm, follows immediately after 118, together with the Psalms of Ascents which I have elsewhere interpreted as an autumn pilgrimage sequence. When we come to look at classic reconstructions of Psalms liturgies by major figures such as Mowinckel and Johnson, we will see that the autumn festival has proved to be a favourite location for a whole variety of possible events.

One final comment: is it significant that almost all the psalms which we have at least tentatively associated with Passover and Sukkot belong to the later books od Psalms, predominantly IV and V, with a few in III?

3. Liturgical indications in individual psalms

That this question needs to be put is a recognition of the widespread belief, traceable at least to Gunkel, that a significant number, if not the majority of the psalms as we now have them are in the service of individual piety rather than any cultic use. Gunkel and Mowinckel occupy perhaps opposite extremes of that spectrum, but it certainly poses problems for the recovery of formal liturgical evidence. The use of refrains and repetitions, and the presence of what appear to be formulae of blessing or invocation, may not be original, but either a later development, or the imitation of familiar public forms in private prayer. My approach will err on the generous side, on the assumption that imitation and reuse are in effect indirect evidence for actual cultic forms.

There are a number of psalms which seem to imply a procession, proof (if we need it) that processions or stylized pilgrimages were part of regular worship. This is implied by the requirement that all males appear before God three times a year, and explicit in Zech.

14.16, though there the context is eschatological, with all the nations '[going] up year by year to worship the King, the Lord of hosts'. Both in this case, and in Deut. 31.10-11 where 'all Israel' is instructed to 'appear before the Lord your God at the place that he will choose', it is Sukkot that is referred to. If (as I have argued in connection with the Psalms of Ascents) Sukkot was also associated with a celebration of the bringing of the ark to Jerusalem, then David's notorious dancing procession in 2 Sam. 6.12-15 is another piece in the jigsaw. To this we might add those late psalms which emphasize the use of musical instruments and joyful singing as a key part of the worship of Yahweh. No doubt this is in some sense a rather trivial conclusion; but not all festivals involve processions, and not all processions require musical accompaniment; nor do all include dancing: for an instance in the Psalms, see 30.11.

Among the psalms which imply a procession we may count 15 and 24 (both including what is often described as an 'entrance liturgy': 15 *in toto* and 24.3-6); the reference to a procession in 42.4 (cf. 55.14); the vivid language of Psalm 47 which has similarities with both Psalm 24 and the 'enthronement of Yahweh' psalms with which it is normally included (93; 95–99), a group of psalms often cited as the core of an autumnal festival celebrating the kingship of Yahweh. One of the great processional psalms, comparable with 24; 118; and 132, is Psalm 68, a psalm which can readily be associated with the warrior God of the ark, and which includes one of the most explicit descriptions we have of the shape of a procession (vv. 24-27):

> Your solemn processions are seen, O God,
>   the processions of my God, my king, into the sanctuary –
> the singers in front, the musicians last,
>   between them girls playing tambourines:
> 'Bless God in the great congregation,
>   the Lord, O you who are of Israel's fountain!'
> There is Benjamin, the least of them, in the lead,
>   the princes of Judah in a body,
>   the princes of Zebulun, the princes of Naphtali.

Psalm 100 also suggests a procession, if 'Enter his gates with thanksgiving, and his courts with praise' is more than an invitation to individual attendance at the ritual; certainly it has inspired one of the most popular of the metrical versions, 'All people that on earth do dwell', especially set to the tune of 'The Old 100th'.

A number of psalms include refrains, or strongly suggest antiphonal performance through the use of a variety of voices. Psalm 136, which opens and closes with the same formula ('O give thanks to X, for he is good,/ for his steadfast love endures for ever' three times at the beginning and once at the end, with a different value for X on each occasion), and repeats the second line of the formula after every subsequent statement of God's great work, is a classic example. Another similar case is Psalm 150, which opens and closes with the simple exclamation 'Praise the Lord!' (*hallelujah*), between which there is a litany of praises of various kinds. Incidentally, this is one of a number of psalms which make it clear that a range of musical instruments was deployed in worship; see also 47.5; 68.25; 71.22; 92.3; 98.5-6; and 108.2. Further examples of refrains are to be found, for example in Psalm 8 which opens and closes with the same words, and psalms with internal refrains such as Psalm 80 in which the formula 'Restore us, X, that we may be saved' is found at vv. 3, 7 and 19, or Psalms 9/10 in which we find 'Rise up O God' at 9.19 and 10.12, or Psalms 42/43 in which the refrain 'Why are you cast down. O my soul ...' is found three times (42.5, 11; 43.5). Evidence for the use of different voices is easy to find; Psalms 24; 121; and 132 are but three examples where this phenomenon is particularly clear.

Liturgical formulae also abound, from the very simple *hallelujah*, to the more elaborate 'O give thanks to the Lord,/ for his steadfast love endures for ever' (136.1 etc.), to the complex 'The Lord is gracious and merciful,/ slow to anger and abounding in steadfast love./ The Lord is good to all,/ and his compassion is over all that he has made' (145.8-9). While it would be possible to provide a fairly comprehensive list, there seems little point in doing so here, since the existence of these formulae is indisputable, their distribution widespread, and their function as congregational responses highly probable.

4. Liturgical settings elsewhere in the Old Testament

Although, as we have seen above, there are a number of festival and liturgical occasions within the Old Testament, few of them give us direct evidence for the use of psalms. References to the practice of the festivals are conveniently set out in Table 5.2. Perhaps the most puzzling feature of this list is that in no case is any liturgical material included. The case we made above for a possible connection between specific psalms and the festivals of Passover or Booths is entirely secondary, and cannot be directly demonstrated through biblical usage. This is most surprising in relation to Chronicles, for there at least we know that certain psalms are cited in what seem to be worship situations. At the end of Chapter 3 we noted briefly J.W. Watts's monograph on the use of psalm-like material in narrative contexts; apart from Exodus 15, which we have noted above in connection with Passover, most of these are not helpful in addressing our present dilemma.

However, there are two contexts which merit further consideration: the use of specific psalms in Chronicles, and evidence for formulae in Numbers which may have become incorporated in psalms. The cry 'Arise, O Lord!' in Num. 10.35, which is there associated with the ark, is found (in various forms) several times in the Psalms (3.7; 7.6; 9.19; 10.12; 17.13; 68.1; 102.13; 132.3). In two of these – Psalms 68 and 132 – there are explicit or implicit references to the ark, prompting the speculation that there may have been some kind of liturgy associated with that sacred object. The so-called Aaronic blessing in Num. 6.24-26 is made up of resonant phrases which can be found in the Psalms; the fact that there is evidence that it existed as a separate blessing (see the discussion of the silver amulet in Chapter 3) may be of significance, though it does not take us very far in the direction of any particular liturgical usage.

It is well known that Chronicles makes use of a group of psalms from Book IV in an overtly liturgical context; and while we have no way of knowing whether this is a report of normal practice or an illustrative use of typical material, the fact that such psalms are used and that they are drawn from Book IV is interesting. There are also shorter allusions to Psalm 132, though whether they require knowledge of the complete psalm or indeed of the Psalms of Ascents as a whole is more doubtful. Table 3 provides a list of Psalms citations in Chronicles and Ezra in what appear to be liturgical situations.

Table 5.3 Psalms cited liturgically in Chronicles and Ezra

Bible	Psalm		Psalm	Bible
1 Chron. 16.8-22	105.1-15		96.1-13	1 Chron. 16.23-33
1 Chron. 16.23-33	96.1-13		105.1-15	1 Chron. 16.8-22
1 Chron. 16.34	106.1		106.1*	1 Chron. 16.34; 2 Chron. 5.13b; 7.3-6; 20.31; Ezra 3.11
1 Chron. 16.35-36	106.47-48		106.47-48	1 Chron. 16.35-36
1 Chron. 28.2	132.7			
2 Chron. 5.13b	106.1			

2 Chron. 6.41-42	132.8-10		132.7	1 Chron. 28.2
2 Chron. 7.3-6	106.1			
2 Chron. 20.21	106.1		132.8-10	2 Chron. 6.41-42
Ezra 3.11	106.1			

*Note: The words of Ps. 106.1 also appear in Pss. 107.1; 118.1, 29; and 136.1. It is perhaps misleading to link them specifically to Psalm 106. That specific connection is, however, reinforced by the fact that 106.47-48 are also cited in the same Chronicles passage. The citation in Ezra 3.11 is perhaps only that of a familiar formula.

The long hymn of thanksgiving which forms the bulk of 1 Chronicles 16 belongs to a description of the ceremony in which the ark of the covenant was brought to Jerusalem in the reign of David. It represents, therefore, a one-off historical event rather than a regular liturgical performance – though there is a case to be made for the existence of some such festival in post-exilic times. Unfortunately, the wider context of 1 Chron. 15.1–16.8 and 16.37-43 gives no clue as to the time of year when this event took place, and the psalms quoted (96; 105; and 106) have no titles. However, 2 Chron. 5.2–7.10 provides a long account of a subsequent ceremony in which Solomon placed the ark in the newly constructed sanctuary. In this account specific dates are given (see in particular 2 Chron. 5.7 and 7.8-10) which make it absolutely clear that the ceremony took place at Sukkot and concluded on the 23rd day of the month when Solomon 'sent the people away to their homes, joyful and in good spirits'. The echo (or anticipation) of *simchat torah* (the modern Jewish festival which celebrates the end of the liturgical year) is suggestive, and may be compared with the similar mood in Psalm 126 where again the season of the autumn harvest is indicated. The directions provided for the performance of the psalm in 1 Chronicles 16 state that 'on that day David first appointed that thanksgiving be sung to the Lord by Asaph and his brethren'. At the end of the psalm we read that 'David left Asaph and his brethren there before the ark of the covenant of the Lord to minister continually before the ark as each day required' – implying the existence of a continuing ceremonial on a daily basis, though it is somewhat odd that the psalms which the Chroniclers associate explicitly with Asaph include none of those which are attributed to Asaph in the Psalter.

The use of this small group of psalms in the context of an ark liturgy is interesting, if not diagnostic. There are few specific motifs within 96 and 105 which would suggest any close connection to the ark (24; 68; and 132 would be better choices in that respect – and indeed, the last of these seems to be referred to in the later ceremony in 2 Chron. 6.41-42) – the two which most obviously suggest themselves are the motif of 'Yahweh is king' (96.10, and perhaps 105.14, 'he rebuked kings on their account') and the use of a word for God's power in 96.7 and 105.4 which is elsewhere closely associated with the power of the ark. That the choice in 1 Chronicles 16 is confined to Book IV *may* be significant, in that this might just hint at the possibility that it was that part of the developing Psalter which was in current use at the time of writing. Given the fairly clear indication that the Chroniclers have made use of a written form of Psalm 106 together with 105 and 96, it does not seem unreasonable to conclude that we have evidence here for a living liturgy within the second-temple cult.

The other psalm which is directly referenced is Psalm 132. There is an explicit quotation in 2 Chron. 6.41-42 (Solomon's ceremonial transfer of the ark to the temple) which cites vv. 1, 8-10 of the psalm, and there is a further reference in 1 Chron. 28.2 in the setting of David's handover of power to Solomon. The latter reads: 'I had planned to build a *house* of *rest* for the *ark* of the *covenant* of the Lord, for the *footstool* of our God; and I made preparations for building.' The words emphasized here constitute verbal links with Psalm 132 which are sufficient to suggest strongly the possibility of a direct quotation. The combination of the specific term for 'rest' found in Ps. 132.7-8 with the reference to the ark and the footstool is unique to these two verses. However, the psalm does not use the phrase 'house of rest' as such, and while it does mention 'my covenant' it does not explicitly refer to 'the ark of the covenant'. On the other hand, there is another well-known context in which the ark and the same term for 'rest' are combined – Num. 10.33-35 – a passage which seems to preserve a traditional formulation about the military importance of the ark. What we have, therefore, is a threefold intertextual link in which the most likely primary source (Numbers) may have contributed to each of the others independently, or to one and then the other, but not in any identifiable order.

In 2 Chron. 6.41-42 we find a passage which is curiously similar to Ps. 132.8-10. The differences are significant, however, and it seems unlikely that either source used a *written* copy of the other. On balance, the likeliest explanation is to be found in a shared use of a familiar piece of liturgy – no doubt associated with the ceremony of the ark whose existence is suggested by Chronicles. Here too the passage from Numbers 10 may have had a part to play. This finding is strengthened by the clear evidence, already noted in our discussion of 1 Chronicles 16, that the Chroniclers were perfectly capable of copying a very closely similar version of existing psalms into their text.

5. Festivals and liturgies in the ancient Near East

Clearly Israel was not an isolated entity in the ancient Near East, even if we need to be wary of assuming parity with societies like Egypt, Babylon and Assyria. Its closest links were almost certainly with Canaanite and Phoenician cultures with which it shared much in the way of language, mythology and cultic practice. Tracing precise influence is, however, more difficult. The impressive mythological texts from Ugarit, for example, are written in a language similar to Hebrew and refer to gods and monsters whose names appear also in the Old Testament. But the gap in time between the destruction of Ugarit and the likely composition of any of the psalms (at least 300 years) means that we cannot draw direct lines of communication. We can, however, appeal to the conservatism of ancient society, a slower pace of language development than in modern times, and the persistence of mythic stories, to argue that there is a commonality of tone and cultic tradition.

It is not possible to discuss this in detail here, but a few examples might be of interest. Perhaps the most famous parallel is that which many commentators have detected between Akhenaten's 'Hymn to the Aten' (fourteenth century BCE) and Psalm 104. It is not clear how such a comparison is to be handled, if there is indeed textual dependence. Perhaps the simplest solution would be, recognizing that Psalm 104 is a late composition, that the writer was able to use a popular edition of Aten: but this is obviously very speculative. Some of the parallels, for what they are worth, are listed in Table 5.4 (Beyerlin 1978: 16–19). Readers are invited to make their own judgements about the closeness or otherwise of the parallels.

Table 5.4

	Hymn to Aten		Psalm 104
lines 3–4	Although you are far away, your rays are on earth; ... When you set on the western horizon, the earth lies in darkness as in death. ... Every lion has come forth from its den, and all the snakes bite	vv. 20-21	You make darkness, and it is night, when all the animals of the forest come creeping out. The young lions roar for their prey.
line 6	The ships sail upstream and down, every way is open because you appear. The fish in the river dart before your face, for your rays penetrate into the depths of the sea.	vv. 25-26	Yonder is the sea, great and wide, creeping things innumerable are there, living things both small and great. There go the ships, and Leviathan that you formed to sport in it.
lines 9–10	You have set a Nile in heaven, and it comes down for them; it makes waves on the mountains like a sea, to water their fields by their settlements. ... Your rays make all plants grow tall: when you rise, they live and grow for you.	vv.10, 13-14	You make springs gush forth in the valleys; they flow between the hills... From your lofty abode you water the mountains; the earth is satisfied with the fruit of your work. You cause the grass to grow for the cattle, ...

Another composition, this time from Canaan, is from the Ugaritic prayer to El and the assembly of the gods (thirteenth century BCE; Beyerlin 1978: 222), which has often been compared with Psalm 29:

O El! O sons of El!
O assembly of the sons of El!
O meeting of the sons of El!
   Be gracious, O El!
   Be a support, O El!
   Be salvation, O El!
   O El, hasten, come swiftly!
   To the help of Zaphon,
    to the help of Ugarit.
Because of the burnt offering, O El,
because of the appointed sacrifice, O El,
because of the morning sacrifice, O El.

The similarities this time are more to do with the structure and form of the piece, than with its content, in the threefold invocation. If this (or a piece like it) did indeed influence Psalm 29, it proved very influential, for its style and traces of its content can be found in the enthronement psalms of Yahweh in Book IV; and in particular, in Psalm 96.

While individual compositions from Hittite sources and from Mesopotamia have been examined intensively for what they might teach us about Israelite psalmody, most of these studies are quite technical, and difficult to summarize. Work has been done, for example, on royal Hittite prayers in time of sickness, plague or famine, drawing out similarities and differences; and from a different perspective, Roger Tomes (2005) has recently produced a fascinating study of how letters from suppliants to the king in the ancient Near East reflect similar circumstances to those psalms in which the psalmist pleads to God for mercy. But the principal influence of the Mesopotamian material in general, and of Babylon in particular, has been on interpretations of the Israelite autumn festival. They have encouraged scholars to see it as the manifestation of an enthronement rite in which both Yahweh and the king were held to have participated, and which at some stage included a celebration of the covenant based on Torah. The main proponents of these reconstructions are Mowinckel (1962), Johnson (1955 [1962]), and Weiser (1962). More recently John Day (1990: 67-87) has provided a succinct overview of these theories with a useful bibliography, to which the reader is directed. I shall review Mowinckel, Weiser and Johnson briefly in concluding this consideration of the wider influence of liturgical compositions in the ancient Near East.

a. Mowinckel

The first of these is the best known, and Mowinckel remains the name that springs immediately to mind when the autumn enthronement festival is mentioned. The basis for his reconstruction lay in three observations: that there is undoubtedly a cultic dimension to the Psalms; that there was certainly a major autumn New Year festival in Israel; and that we know of an enthronement festival from other sources, most particularly Babylon. The detailed case he presents can be found in the chapter of his major work entitled 'Psalms at the Enthronement Festival of Yahweh' (Mowinckel 1962: I, 106-92). Mowinckel weaves together a matrix of interlocking evidence to support his argument. The story begins with the group of 'Enthronement of Yahweh' psalms which have long been regarded as belonging together – 47; 93; and 96–99. To these he adds 95 and, in parallel with it, 81. The central ideas in these psalms are: the role of creation, the defeat of other gods, and the establishment of Israel. Moreover the language indicates an ongoing, present event ('Yahweh is/has become king') which surely suggests a familiar ritual. There will have been a great festal procession associated with the enthronement, and here it is plausible to bring in Psalms 24 and 132, both of which were associated with the ark, and in all probability part of this procession.

As to the date of this ceremony, the major festival in ancient times was undoubtedly Sukkot. Several psalms can be certainly linked with Sukkot – 65; 67; and 118 being the most obvious. Mowinckel further argues that Psalm 81, which he has already identified as very similar to Psalm 95 and to be included with the enthronement psalms, is a new year psalm (the clearest indication is the reference to wheat in the last verse; it might be objected that in other terms there are more obvious associations with Passover (thus vv. 4-7). There is thus a cluster of significant processional psalms associated with Sukkot, something we have noted already above; and these, according to Mowinckel, can be further linked with the enthronement psalms.

Finally, Mowinckel draws on other ancient Near Eastern practice to provide parallels to the rite of royal enthronement. There is evidence, for example, of the enthronement of Baal after his resurrection and victory over Mot (the god of death) (Mowinckel 1962: I, 125), and the ceremonies in Babylon at the new year when Marduk was enthroned, while not perhaps providing a direct influence, show a commonality of theme which enables us to place the Israelite rite in a wider context (I, 130–40 *passim*).

b. Johnson

Johnson's best-known work remains *Sacral Kingship in Ancient Israel*, first published in 1955, with a second edition in 1962. In it he takes the enthronement theme further by focusing on both the enthronement psalms and the royal psalms, and drawing from them evidence for an elaborate ritual combining cosmogony – a celebration of Yahweh's victory over chaos, his enthronement above all the gods, and his creative power – and eschatology, in the form of a drama in which those participating are assured of victory over death, called to a renewal of faith, and challenged to be obedient in order that the new order of righteousness and peace might be recognized (Johnson 1955 [1962]: 101–02). A particular feature of his reconstruction is the identification of a trial in which the king participated, undergoing a ritual humiliation similar to that of the king in the Babylonian festival (Johnson 1955 [1962]: 102–28). The argument is based on a detailed exegesis of Psalm 89, in particular vv. 38-45, from which he draws the following conclusion:

> Thus we see that at this autumnal festival the Davidic king, for all that he is the specially chosen Servant of the omnipotent, heavenly King, is a suffering Servant. He is the Messiah of Yahweh; but on this occasion, at least, he is a humble Messiah. What we see, however, is a ritual humiliation which in principle is not unlike that suffered by the Babylonian king in the analogous New Year Festival. (1955 [1962]: 113)

This is not an easy book to read, and the specific case is argued on the basis of a very detailed exegesis of the relevant psalms which may not now be sustainable. Nevertheless it represents an impressive and important stage on the quest for a satisfactory cultic rationale for the Psalms.

c. Weiser

Artur Weiser's commentary first appeared in 1935; the fifth edition of 1959 was translated in 1962 and published in the SCM Old Testament Library series. Weiser's thesis concerning existence of a covenant festival at new year was first set out in the third edition of 1949. He assumes a largely pre-exilic date for the majority of the psalms, and interprets them as having been composed for a cult of the covenant which originated with the tribal confederacy, and became under the monarchy a covenant festival of Yahweh.

Weiser understands this festival to have taken the form of a cultic drama in which the congregation re-enacted the Sinai covenant. A theophanic appearance symbolized by the ark lay at its heart. With the development of the monarchy, ideas of enthronement and the role of the king gradually merged with the original festival, which ultimately acquired a messianic dimension in the post-exilic period (Weiser 1962: 23-35; see also 35-52 for a discussion of the place of specific psalms in the festival). It must be said that Weiser's thesis has little modern support. The significance of the covenant as a defining motif in the Old Testament would not now so readily be associated with the pre-monarchic or even monarchic periods, and is more likely to be seen as a Deuteronomistic innovation (or emphasis), symbolized for example in the reading of the law at Sukkot every seventh year in Deut. 31.9-13.

6. The Mishnah and the New Testament

The final task we must undertake is to see what we can glean from the immediate successors of the second-temple liturgy: the Mishnah and the New Testament. Holladay (1993: 139-46) provides a brief discussion of the use of the Psalms in early Jewish liturgy, and covers Christian use in an earlier chapter (1993: 113-33). I would like at this point also to note the work of a now forgotten scholar, C.C. Keet (mentioned in Chapter 2 for his work on the Psalms of Ascents) whose *A Liturgical Study of the Psalter* (1928) can still teach us much about this subject. Keet has a particular knowledge of and interest in Jewish liturgy, and makes connections in this direction which are still valid (1928: 105-52). As an indication, perhaps, of the cyclical nature of scholarly fashion, Keet is sceptical (as I have been) about the survival of pre-exilic songs (1928: 43 n. 2), and argues for the Maccabean provenance of Psalm 118 (1928: 113-25). *Plus ça change ...*

a. The Mishnah

The Mishnah is the most frustrating of books to have become the successor to and interpreter of the Old Testament for embryonic Rabbinic Judaism. It codifies many things, but with what to a modern view seems to be culpably scant regard for the biblical traditions. However, within its descriptions of the festivals, in the second division (Edot), there are a number of references to the use of psalms. Together with a few scattered references in other places, we gain a useful

– if limited – understanding of how some of the psalms might have functioned in public ceremonies. Table 5.5 sets out this evidence, on the left in the order of the psalms which are cited, and on the right in the order of the tractates of the Mishnah. I have used Danby's classic translation of the Mishnah (1933).

Table 5.5 Liturgical use of psalms in Mishnah

Psalm	Mishnah	Mishnah	Psalm
24	Tamid 7.4		
30.1	Bikkurim 3.4		
48	Tamid 7.4		
81	Tamid 7.4		
82	Tamid 7.4	Hallah 5.15	92.24
92.24 92	Hallah 5.15 Tamid 7.4	Bikkurim 3.4	30.1
93	Tamid 7.4	Pesahim 5.7, 9.3, 10.6	113–18
94	Tamid 7.4	Sukkah 3.9-11, 4.1, 8 Sukkah 4.5	113–18 118.25
102	Taanith 2.3	Rosh ha-Shanah 4.7	113–18
113–18	Pesahim 5.7, 9.3, 10.6 Sukkah 3.9-11, 4.1, 8 Rosh ha-Shanah 4.7 Taanith 4.5 Megillah 2.5 Sotah 5.4	Taanith 2.3 Taanith 3.9 Taanith 4.5	120, 121, 130 136 113–18
118.25	Sukkah 4.5	Megillah 2.5	113–18
120–34	Middoth 2.5	Sotah 5.4	113–18
120	Taanith 2.3	Tamid 7.4	24, 48, 81, 82, 92, 93, 94
121	Taanith 2.3	Middoth 2.5	120–34
130	Taanith 2.3		
136	Taanith 3.9		

Table 5.5 summarizes the Mishnah evidence. Two very preliminary remarks are in order: first, that by a very significant majority, the psalms cited are drawn from Books IV and V (all but five, of which four belong to the set of seven Tamid psalms); and second, that the Hallel (Psalms 113–18) was clearly a ubiquitous collection, sung regularly on a variety of occasions. Danby remarks (1933: 193 n. 11) that the Hallel 'is in keeping only with the more joyous festivals'. While these may be no more than straws in the wind, it is clear in which direction the wind is blowing. Whatever its origins, the Hallel is without doubt a significant liturgical piece within the late second temple and early Mishnaic period; and the emphasis on psalms from the last two books reinforces what the Qumran materials seem to suggest: that these psalms in particular belong to a living context of religious use. By way of a counterpoint, it is important to be clear that I am not implying that Mishnah only *knows* the later books of the Psalter. Far from it: there are psalms citations from all five books, not listed in Table 5.5. These are largely textual citations used to support or justify a legal or practical point, and in contrast with the liturgical situation, they are much more rarely drawn from Books IV and V, as Table 5.6 shows.

Table 5.6 Non-liturgical citations of psalms in Mishnah

Psalm	Mishnah		Psalm (cont'd)	Mishnah (cont'd)
1.1, 5	Abot 3.2, Sanhedrin 10.2		68.27	Berakhot 7.3
12.2	Sotah 9.12		78.38, 54	Makkot 3.14, Abot 6.10
29.11	Uqsin 3.12		82.1	Abot 3.6
33.15	Rosh ha-Shanah 1.2		92.14	Qiddushin 4.14
37.21	Abot 2		106.28	Abodah Zarah 2.3, Abot 3.3
40.3	Miqvaot 9.2		109.18	Shabbat 9.4
50.5	Sanhedrin 10.3		119.79, 99, 126	Abot 6.9, Abot 4.1, Berakhot 9.5
55.13, 24	Abot 6.3, 5.19		128.2	Abot 4.1, 6.4

To summarize: Eleven psalms (fourteen citations) from Books I–III are used for non-liturgical purposes while five psalms (seven citations) are taken from Books IV–V. By contrast, liturgical contexts are found in the case of five psalms (five citations) from Books I–III and 26 (counting six for the Hallel psalms and fifteen for the Songs of Ascent), sixteen citations in all, from Books IV–V. The numbers are small, and there is no statistical significance to be deduced; nevertheless the bias is towards a favouring of Books IV and V for liturgical purposes, with a corresponding sense that the earlier sub-collections are slightly more 'antique' in character – perhaps honoured for the role they once played, but no longer at the forefront of the developing liturgies of the Hasmonaeans, the Pharisees and the early stages of Rabbinic Judaism.

The Hallel in Mishnah

The Hallel Psalms have a prominent place in the prescriptions for Passover, as set out in the Mishnah tractate Pesahim. After the mixing of the second cup, and the question and answer between father and son, the Hallelujah is recited in response to the great redemptive actions commemorated by Passover – both the saving of the firstborn and the escape from Egypt to the promised land as commemorated in the early 'Wandering Aramaean' creed of Deut. 26.5ff. and in the words of Mishnah itself:

> 'Passover' – because God passed over the houses of our fathers in Egypt;
> 'unleavened bread' – because our forefathers were redeemed from Egypt.;
> 'bitter herbs' – because the Egyptians embittered the lives of our fathers in
> Egypt. In every generation a man must so regard himself as if he came forth
> himself out of Egypt ... (M Pesahim 10.5; Danby 1933: 150–51)

The next verse (10.6) reports the famous discussion between Hillel and Shammai about how far the Hallel should be recited at the communal meal – surely in itself indicative of a liturgical process of contemporary interest – while earlier, in 5.7, we learn that the Levites proclaimed the Hallel as often as necessary during the sacrificial ritual. Unlike the citations in chapter 10, this reference supposes the liturgical use of the Hallel far back in history – hardly a surprising claim, but one which is not supported by, for example, the evidence of the Old Testament in which, as we have already seen, there is not a single reference at any point to a psalmic liturgy associated with the feast. We may safely conclude therefore that Mishnah is here romanticizing the past rather than reporting on genuine traditional practice.

The Hallel also has an important place at the festival of Sukkot, with a special emphasis on the processional Psalm 118 which forms

the climax of that group. Thus M Sukkah 3.9 provides a rubric for
the shaking of the *lulav* (a willow or palm branch) at the beginning
and end of that psalm, and also at verse 25 ('Save us, we beseech you,
O Lord! / O Lord, we beseech you, give us success'). Immediately
after that verse there is to be found the explicit reference to the festal
procession which characterizes this psalm, and which was famously
deployed by the Gospel tradition to describe Jesus's entry into
Jerusalem. Even more explicitly, M Sukkah 4.5 describes a procession
seven times round the altar accompanied with the waving of willow
branches and the recital of v. 25. There can be little doubt that Psalm
118 was a key liturgical item in the celebration of Sukkot as recorded
in Mishnah. The Hallel as a whole is also featured (thus M Sukkah
4.1, 8), and was clearly an important part of the proceedings for the
whole period of the festival. Yet once again we find no echo of this
in the records of the festivals in Tanakh, nor indeed are any other
psalmic materials found in that connection.

There is a somewhat unclear reference to the Hallel in connection
with New Year in M Rosh ha-Shanah 4.7, which could be read as
saying that it is not a necessary part of that festival, but is used
if other factors are present. A passing reference in M Taanith 4.5
records its use on 1st Tebet, towards the end of Hanukkah, and M
Megillah 2.5 records that the Hallel (along with many other prayers
and ceremonies) is appropriate to daylight use. These notes add little
more to our investigation, but certainly confirm the centrality of the
Hallel as a major liturgical item in Jewish practice of the period.

One other point of some note is the indication that it was usual to
have a responsive performance of the Hallel. Thus M Sukkah 3.10,
'If a slave, a woman, or a minor recited [the Hallel] to him he must
repeat after them what they say' and M Sotah 5.4 'It teaches us that
Israel made answer to every thing after Moses, like as when they recite
the Hallel.'

The Songs of Ascents in Mishnah

Despite the attention which a number of scholars have paid to this
group, Mishnah gives us very little to go on, beyond the well-known
account in M Middoth 2.5 of the association of the fifteen Songs
of Ascents with the fifteen steps from the Israelite courtyard to the
women's court in the temple. Whether this means that the songs
were *sung* on these steps is not entirely clear, and no information is
given which would help us to determine whether they were sung at
a particular time of the year, the week, or the day. There is a hint

– no more – in M *Taanit* 2.3 which uses three of these psalms (120; 121; and 130) together with Psalm 102; 1 Kgs 8.37ff.; and Jer. 14.1ff. in connection with blessings recited at the beginning of the days of fasting. While it is not explicit in the text, it seems probable that the 'days of awe' associated with Yom Kippur are covered by this rubric. While this does not associate the Ascents *as a group* with Yom Kippur, it does leave open a broader link with the range of autumn festivals, a link supported by some of the agricultural imagery in, for example, Psalm 126.

Other psalms in Mishnah

In M *Taanith* 3.9, there is a report to the effect that once in Lydda the Great Hallel (Psalm 136) was recited in the afternoon – a reference which is admittedly of little use in establishing any regular liturgical function for the psalm! Other scattered references which indicate liturgical use are to be found in M *Hallah* 5.15 (Ps. 92.24 – the reference is to the cancellation of the singing of this 'psalm of awakening') and M *Bikkurim* 3.4 (Ps. 30.1 – a usage at the festival of the first fruits). Finally, in M *Tamid* 7.4 we are given a list of seven psalms (24; 48; 82; 94; 81; 93; and 92) to be sung on each of the seven days of the week. We have already remarked on Peter L. Trudinger's detailed study of the liturgy of this service, which is of particular interest for being the only place where any psalms outside Books IV and V have a clearly established liturgical role. Unfortunately it is impossible to trace any pre-Mishnaic evidence for the liturgical use of this sequence.

b. The New Testament

If Mishnah is frustrating in its manner of engagement with Tanakh, and its eschewal of anything that looks like (historical) narrative or theology, the New Testament is by contrast tantalizing in that it seems to offer a plethora of such evidence, but largely fails to deliver, at least in terms of our quest for understanding of the Psalms at the time of its composition. Despite the ubiquity of liturgical contexts (visits to the synagogue and the temple, and worship situations within the early Christian community) we find curiously little that might explain what role psalms might have had. That they *did* play a part seems both intuitively obvious and historically plausible – at least in terms of the use of psalms in Christian liturgies of the next few centuries: see, for example, Robert F. Taft, 'Christian Liturgical Psalmody' (Attridge and Fassler 2003: 7–32). But the New Testament itself is curiously vague, and its generalized references to the singing of 'hymns', 'psalms' and 'songs' (Mt. 26.30; 1 Cor. 14.26; Eph. 5.19; Col. 3.16; Jas 5.13; Rev. 5.9; 14.3; 15.3) do not take us very far. Indeed, in the two passages in Revelation where explicit liturgical pieces are reported together with the 'new song' motif (5.9 and 15.3) there are only the vaguest references to existing psalms. NRSV (Manser 2003) cross-references Rev. 5.9 to Ps. 33.3 – but the link turns only on the reference to a 'new song' and has no bearing on the *content* of the song. Links are also proposed between Rev. 15.3 and Ps. 145.17 and between Rev. 15.4 and Ps. 86.8-9. The former connects 'Just and true are thy ways,/ O King of the ages' with 'The Lord is just in all his ways/ and kind in all his doings' – hardly more than an allusion, if that – while the latter depends on a reference to the nations coming to worship and glorify God found in both passages. Again, the two are not verbally close, and the ideas are hardly unique. Further, it is clear that many of the obviously hymnic or liturgical passages in Revelation are either unique (in biblical terms) to that book, echo a variety of Old Testament sources, or depend upon the likes of Isa. 6.2-3. When we take into account also the songs Luke composed for his infancy narrative, which are clearly modelled on Old Testament forms but do not directly quote them, what emerges is the sense of a community (or communities) familiar with the psalms as a body of traditional praise, but largely free to shape their own liturgical traditions in the manner of, but not in slavish imitation of the older materials. Since, unlike Mishnah, the New Testament does not provide liturgical instructions as such, it is difficult to assess the significance of the absence of psalmic material. It could be that there was no need to record, in the course of narrative, usages familiar to the likely readers within the Jewish and Jewish-Christian communities; and no relevance in doing so for gentile congregations. But there are two New Testament contexts which somewhat modify this kind of explanation: first, the clear references to Psalm 118 in the quasi-liturgical setting of the entry into Jerusalem, and second, the fact that Revelation *does* contain liturgical material and is almost certainly (in view of its intensely apocalyptic language) directed to an audience versed in Jewish literary styles, yet nonetheless fails to record whatever traditional Psalms liturgy might have been in use.

In order to enable us to make a more precise evaluation of the role and significance of Psalms in the New Testament and to see whether anything of significance for our study of the Psalms and liturgy can be identified, Table 5.7 provides structured lists of the relevant evidence.

The first lists those passages from various psalms which are directly cited as proof of the meaningfulness of episodes in Jesus's life or in defence of theological positions. The second and third constitute two further lists of more directly liturgical passages, both those which in some way refer to existing psalms, and those which represent the New Testament's own liturgical developments. At the very crudest level of generality it is noteworthy that the broad emphasis reverses that found in Mishnah, as set out in Tables 5.5 and 5.6, in at least two ways: in the weight given to liturgical use, and in the extent to which Books IV and V predominate in Mishnah, but not in the New Testament.

Table 5.7 Psalms in the New Testament

I: Psalms As Theological Proof Texts

2.1-2	Ø	Acts 4.25-26
2.7		Mt. 3.17; 17.5; Mk 1.11; Lk. 3.22; Acts 13.33; Heb. 1.5
5.9	D	Rom. 3.13
8.2	D	Mt. 21.16
8.4-6		Heb. 2.6-9
10.7	Ø	Rom. 3.14
14.1-3	D	Rom. 3.10-12
= 53.1-3		
16.8-11	D	Acts 2.25-28; 13.35
18.49	D	Rom. 15.9
19.4	D	Rom. 10.18
22.1	D	Mt. 27.46; Mk 15.34
22.7-8		Mt. 27.39; Mk 15.31
22.18		Mt. 27.35; Mk 15.24; Lk. 23.34; Jn 19.24
22.22		Heb. 2.12
24.1	D	1 Cor. 10.26
31.5	D	Lk. 23.46
32.1-2	D	Rom. 4.7
34.12-16	D	1 Pet. 3.10-12
35.19	D	Jn 15.25
36.1	D	Rom. 3.18
37.11	D	Mt.5.5
40.6-8	D	Heb. 10.5-9

Table 5.7 (continued)

41.9	D	Jn 13.18
44.22	K	Rom. 8.36
45.6-7	K	Heb. 1.8-9
51.4	D	Rom. 3.4
68.18	D	Eph. 4.8
69.4 69.9 69.22-23 69.25	D	Jn 15.25 Jn 2.17; Rom 15.3 Rom. 11.9 Acts 1.20
78.2	A	Mt. 13.35
82.6	A	Jn 10.34
91.11-12	Ø	Mt. 4.6; Lk. 4.10-11
94.11	Ø	1 Cor. 3.20
95.7-11	Ø	Heb. 3.7-11, 15; 4.3, 5, 7
102.25-27	Ø	Heb. 1.10-12
104.4	Ø	Heb. 1.7
109.8	D	Acts 1.20
110.1 110.4	D	Mt. 22.44; Mk 12.36; Lk. 20.41-44; Acts 2.34-35; Heb. 1.13 Heb. 5.6, 10; 6.20; 7.11, 15, 17, 21, 28
112.9	Ø	2 Cor. 9.9
117.1	Ø	Rom. 15.11
118.6 118.22-23 118.26	Ø	Heb. 13.6 Mt. 21.42; Mk 12.10-11; Lk. 20.17; Acts 4.11; 1 Pet. 2.4, 7 Mt. 23.39; Lk. 13.35
140.3	D	Rom. 3.13

Note: Key to titles: D = David, A = Asaph, K = Korah, Ø = No title.

II: Psalms Used in Liturgical Contexts

2.1	Rev. 11.18
23.2	Rev. 7.17
118.26	Mt. 21.9; Mk 11.9; Lk. 19.38; Jn 12.13
121.6	Rev. 7.16

Table 5.7 (continued)

III: Other Liturgical Material

Beatitudes	
	Mt. 5.3-12; Lk. 6.20-26
Lord's Prayer	
	Mt. 6.9-13; Lk. 11.2-4
Passover/Eucharist	
	Mt. 26.20-30; Mk 14.17-26; Lk. 22.14-23, 39; 1 Cor. 11.23-26
Infancy Songs	
	Lk. 1.14-17, 32-35, 46-55, 68-79; 2.29-35
Commission & Blessing	
	Mt. 28.18-20; Rom. 16.25-27
Kenosis	
	Phil. 2.5-11
By faith ...	
	Heb. 11
Miscellaneous Hymns	
	Rev. 4.8, 11; 5.9-14; 7.15-17; 11.17-18; 14.13; 15.3-4; 19.1-8; 21.3-8

Note: Key to titles: D = David, A = Asaph, K = Korah, Ø = No title.

Liturgical uses

Though three instances are given from Revelation, it must be admitted
that they are all in fact little more than fragmentary allusions to
familiar phrases, and scarcely count as direct evidence of liturgical
use of psalms in the New Testament. As we have already observed,
given the considerable extent to which liturgy is present in that book
this is a surprising finding which must count as negative information
of some importance in our overview of the historical context within
which psalms functioned in the first century CE. Assuming that the
book of Revelation (whatever its ultimate origins in apocalyptic)
appears to be located within a situation of persecution, it may be that
its silence on psalmic liturgy is a deliberate response to the need for
the target audience to create a distinctive and aggressive self-identity
independent of its older roots. On the other hand, a much simpler
– though in many ways more radical – conclusion would be that there

was no strong liturgical tradition to which the writer of Revelation could appeal, beyond the *models* provided in the Old Testament. If it is legitimate to match the difference in dating of the New Testament and Mishnah (broadly speaking, late first century for the former, late second for the latter) with their different reporting of psalms as liturgy, it might follow that some of what we see in Mishnah represents ways in which the use of the Psalms was developing in the Rabbinic era immediately after the destruction of the temple.

The only other clear liturgical use of psalms in the New Testament is that associated with what Christians call 'Palm Sunday' – a single motif found in all four canonical Gospels. Even this does not constitute direct evidence, but is rather the application of what appears to be one popular aspect of a festal procession to the specific historical occasion of Jesus's entry into Jerusalem. This is problematic for our purposes, since the psalm itself seems to be applied to Sukkot in Mishnah while the Gospel traditions unequivocally relate the entry to a few days before Passover. Doubt has sometimes been cast on the Passover timing of the 'triumphal entry' on the grounds that the parable of the fig tree, which is variously recorded in the synoptics, would make much more sense at the time of the autumn festival when the tree could have been expected to bear fruit. This raises the possibility that the time between Jesus's entry to Jerusalem and the events of Passover the following year has been collapsed into a single dramatic story by the tradition. In any event, it turns out that the one strongly liturgical psalmic piece in the New Testament can tell us little or nothing about the writers' familiarity with any extant Jewish practice.

Theological proof texts

At least 36 different psalms are explicitly quoted or referred to in connection with the desire of New Testament writers to support their case, consisting of over eighty individual citations (synoptic citations are counted separately). These figures are not precise because of a degree of uncertainty where reference shades into allusion. I have erred on the side of caution – thus the figures given may under-represent the extent to which New Testament authors used psalms to support their arguments.

Table 5.8 Distribution of psalms as proof texts in the New Testament

	No. of Psalms Cited	% of total in that book	No. of citations	% of total (83)	Prominent psalms
Book I (1–41)	18	43.9	35	42.2	2, 8, 22
Book II (42–72)	5	16.1	9	10.8	69
Book III (73–89)	2	11.7	2	2.4	
Book IV (90–106)	5	29.4	12	14.5	
Book V (107–150)	6	13.6	25	30.1	110, 118

The psalms cited are drawn, though not evenly, from all five books – the distributions are shown in the table – but six individual psalms seem to have had a more prominent role (2, 8, 22, 69, 110 and 118), representing between them 46 (55.4%) of the total number of citations. No discernible pattern emerges beyond the cautious statement that Books I and V appear to attract somewhat more attention. If this has any significance, it might be attributed to two factors: first, that Book I is the primary Davidic collection, and second, that Book V might represent the most active context in liturgical use. Regarding the first point, we have already seen that the Qumran community – like the Christian, focused in particular on the person of the Davidic messiah – seems to have emphasized the Davidic character of the Psalms. We might also note that all of the group of six which are cited more frequently are either Davidic or untitled (2 and 118); and of the cited psalms as a whole, twenty-two are Davidic, ten are untitled (and of these, Psalm 10 is often combined with the Davidic Psalm 9), and just four have other attributions (44 and 45 to Korah and 78 and 82 to Asaph). While this might suggest a tendency to avoid psalms explicitly attributed to others than David it hardly constitutes strong evidence. The second point is seriously weakened by the fact that we have already noted a surprising lack of reference in the pages of the New Testament to the liturgical use of the Psalms. If the New Testament as a whole has almost no interest in the Psalms as liturgy, it cannot be claimed that such an interest, perversely, lies behind the use of untitled psalms in Book V.

Other liturgies and prayers in the New Testament

The remaining section of Table 5.7 presents the main examples of liturgies in the New Testament. They are of varying kinds: the *rubric* for the eucharist; various *blessings* (including the Beatitudes); *hymns and songs* such as those in the early chapters of Luke, in Revelation, and the kenosis hymn in Philippians; the *litany* of the faithful in Hebrews 11; and the model *intercessory prayer* known as the Lord's Prayer. In different ways, many of these have parallels in Tanakh, deuterocanonical texts or in Jewish liturgical contexts – we noted the parallels between the Lord's Prayer and 1 Chron. 29.10-13 in Chapter 3.

The closest to psalms in form are the various songs Luke composed for his infancy narrative (which is as a whole closely modelled on 1 Samuel 1–3), with Hannah's Song providing an obvious starting point. Similarly, many of the hymns in Revelation sound as though they could have been in the Psalter, though they are in fact distinct compositions. This pattern is reminiscent of the existence at a number of points in the Old Testament of compositions which 'feel' like psalms but are not in the Psalter, such as Hannah's Song (of course), the Song of the Sea in Exodus 15, and Jonah's prayer from the belly of the fish. It might be argued on the basis of this similarity of compositional technique that – while the New Testament writers in the main do not *use* the Psalms liturgically – they were perfectly well aware that they could function in such contexts, but chose to make their own contribution tailored to the needs of the Christian communities.

On the whole, our survey of the New Testament materials has proved largely disappointing in terms of evidence for the use of the Psalms in living religious traditions in the first century. It is clear, nevertheless, that the collection was available and was utilized, both as a means of reinforcing the claims made by Christians for their messiah (especially Psalms 2; 22; 110; and 118 in the Gospels) and – perhaps less overtly – as a model for the shaping of early Christian liturgies. The surprising (though tentative and interim) conclusion we might draw is that *even as regards the use of the Psalms* both Christianity and Judaism appear to be 'feeling their way' in the first century, as though neither has a fixed synagogue liturgy or tradition to appeal to. Such a conclusion would accord with that strand of historical opinion which is reluctant to find formal synagogues (at least in the form of dedicated buildings) at too early a period in Jewish religious history. It would also fit with the likelihood that the destruction of Jerusalem and the temple in 70 CE (followed by the disaster of the Bar Kokhba revolt) were the events which stimulated the development of Rabbinic religion in terms of both legal and liturgical practice. On this view Mishnah is an account not of ancient practice but of recent innovation.

Perhaps the most surprising effect of this is to cast doubt on the place of the Hallel in first-century Judaism. Its only locus in the New Testament is, as we have seen, in the context of a Sukkot-like procession, which is in any case already indicated within Psalm 118 itself. The statement that Jesus and the disciples sang a hymn at the end of the Last Supper is wholly unspecific – in any case, the Pesah ritual involved the *recital* (not the singing) of the Hallel.

7. Conclusion

Much ground has been covered in this chapter, some of it perhaps fruitlessly. What emerges is a paradox: that the Psalms must almost certainly have been put to liturgical use, but with little or no clarity as to what that use might have been. The New Testament is surprisingly unhelpful; Mishnah tells us a little more, but its primary interest is in law rather than liturgy; and what may have gone on in the Temple during any of its incarnations has been (and will no doubt continue to be) the subject of much speculation. If there is any consensus it is that the New Year festival, whatever its theological meaning, had a central place. I would add to that the near certainty that we can identify a body of psalms which would have been appropriate for use at Passover. Beyond these few remarks the rest, regrettably, must be a decent silence.

Chapter 6

Theological, Philosophical and Anthropological Reflections

1. General matters

The mere use of the term 'theology' tends to drive discussion in a certain direction. For many people it implies a Christian discourse, though there is nothing in its etymology which necessitates that understanding, and there are some Jewish thinkers now who are willing to use the term. It also forces a God-centred analysis, as if everything these poems have to tell us is in a single direction. Third, it suggests a systematic hermeneutic which will offer a key to understanding everything in the Psalter. And fourth, it might seem to shut out those of an agnostic or secular instinct who yet find something to warm to in the Psalms. While I recognize that these are all in one way or another over-simplifications of the case, there is still some truth in the implied objections. For that reason I have adopted a somewhat cumbersome title for this chapter, more by way of a deliberate confusing of the boundaries than as a promise of anything systematic or rigorous in any of the three stated respects. The title should be taken as a reminder that the Psalter is open to many different readings by all sorts of people who bring to it a vast range of emotion and experience. How else can we explain, for example, the evocative power of Psalm 23 for thousands of people who have not the remotest connection with either church or synagogue? We saw in a previous chapter how W. L. Holladay uses this cultural phenomenon to bracket his review of the Psalms 'through three thousand years' (Holladay 1993). It is that kind of resonance that I want to explore in this chapter, along with more traditional 'theologies'. There is room here, in short, for Boney M's 'Rivers of Babylon' as well as Bernstein's *Chichester Psalms*.

It would be foolish, of course, to resist the obvious truth that belief in the gods was pretty much ubiquitous in the world of the Israelites. Even the appearance of denial is often misleading, being almost certainly something less than full atheism. The writer of Psalm 14 comes closest, in postulating the fool who imagines that 'God is not'; but for the most part – even for Qoheleth (Ecclesiastes), who deems God to be ineffably distant and impenetrable to the human mind – the concept of atheism was beyond normal discourse. Having said that, we may then regard much of what is expressed as having a human-centred dimension; even God is assumed to have human feelings, to be susceptible to the kind of arguments that would be effective with human tyrants, and to be capable of regrets and indecision. There is, in short, a profoundly humanist accent to the psalmists' prayers, imprecations and petitions, one which may well shed as much light on the society from which these poems emerged as on the nature of the God to whom they are addressed.

2. Jewish contributions

The literature of Psalms interpretation in the academic field is rather dominated by writers of a more or less explicit Christian persuasion. Notable exceptions are Jonathan Magonet (1994), whose 'rabbinic readings' offer an insight into a liberal Jewish understanding, and Nahum Sarna (1993), who offers interpretations from a Jewish perspective on Psalms 1; 8; 15; 19; 24; 30; 48; 82; 93; and 94. Of the two Sarna is the more scholarly, though both are directed at a lay readership. In terms of the poetics of the Psalms, I have had occasion in Chapter 4 to note the important contributions of Fisch (1988) and Alter (1990). In this context it is appropriate also to note Herbert J. Levine (1995), who offers a contemporary reading of the Psalms in his *Sing Unto God a New Song*. The first two chapters deal with methodological questions and provide a setting for the Psalms within temple worship based on the myth-and-ritual school of thought. In the remaining three chapters Levine deals with more explicitly theological questions, discussing 'the conflict between faith and experience, especially as it is manifest in the give-and-take of the Psalms' competing voices', 'the representation of deliverance in the Psalms' (1995: xii), and concluding in his final chapter with an exploration of the Psalms as responses to repeated national catastrophes.

3. Christian theology and the Psalms

Space does not permit a discussion of the rather large number of Christian theological interpretations of the Psalms. I shall restrict myself to a brief report on Anderson (1983), Kraus (1992), McCann (1993b) and Mays (1994), and a more detailed consideration of Westermann (1981) and Brueggemann (1980, 1984).

Bernhard Anderson's *Out of the Depths: The Psalms Speak for Us Today* identifies itself as primarily a handbook for churches. It might be best described as an introduction to the Psalms, broadly based on the classic types, which emphasizes theological and personal aspects of the poems both in Israel and for modern (Christian) readers. Hans-Joachim Kraus, whose major commentary on the Psalms must be considered a companion to his *Theology*, takes a fairly traditional, very detailed approach to his subject. It was originally published in German in 1979, and displays some of the rather forbidding aspects of the kind of scholarship which depends upon a painstakingly thorough examination of every relevant text. His chapters deal with 'The God of Israel', 'The People of God', 'The Sanctuary and Its Worship', 'The King', 'The Enemy Powers', 'The Individual in the Presence of God', and 'The Psalms in the New Testament'. For those who relish an exhaustive treatment of what are certainly fundamental themes, this is an invaluable resource, if a little indigestible. McCann (*A Theological Introduction to the Book of Psalms: The Psalms as Torah*) and Mays (*The Lord Reigns: A Theological Handbook to the Psalms*) focus on specific categories: the former emphasizing the place of Torah as a key to understanding and applying the Psalms, the latter arguing that the 'Yahweh is King' psalms are the central and controlling theological idea for the whole Psalter; an idea, moreover, which can be made theologically relevant to our own time.

a. Westermann

Westermann's *Praise and Lament in the Psalms* consists in the main of an extensive discussion of these two genres (1981: 15–213). It is in the remaining sections of his book that we find significant theological reflection. Westermann begins with some important thoughts on the nature of history as it functions in the Psalms (1981: 214–58):

> The 're-presentation' of history receives its most direct and tangible expression in the Psalms of the lament of the people. The past forces itself into the present precisely in its contrast to the present. What *has* happened

is heard as the antithesis of what *is* happening. ... *God* is confronted with former deeds in order to persuade him to do now, not what he is doing but by contrast what he had done earlier. (1981: 215)

It follows that the re-presentation of history serves the purpose of both reminding the congregation and, by forcing God to remember, influencing contemporary events – events which (for the Israelites) were in direct continuity with God's past activity (1981: 220).

Laments frequently include a vow of praise. This is more than simply a formal undertaking to praise God: it has significance for the understanding of history in the Old Testament:

> The idea of a continuous event, and therewith historical time, is perceived when, in the context of God's relationship to humanity, two points in time are related in the reciprocal relation of word and deed (that is, in the sense of word and response). This is the case when a word spoken by God (a solemn vow uttered as a promise) bridges the time between the moment when the word was spoken and the moment in which it is fulfilled. From the human point of view the vow of praise corresponds to the promise that here, too, the moment of promise creates a tension which lasts until the promise is fulfilled. (1981: 222).

Westermann is clear that this re-presentation does not entail dramatic re-enactions, but is rather a matter of a verbal re-telling, and that not of individual episodes, but of the salvation complex of events which has become known as the *heilsgeschichte*, in order to affirm a relationship between God and God's people (1981: 228).

The book concludes with reflections on the nature of the lament tradition (1981: 259–79). An important characteristic of the lament is that it works in three dimensions: toward God, toward others, and toward the lamenter (1981: 267). This has significance for our understanding of the human condition. Thus:

> The threefold character of the lamentation reveals an understanding of man in which the existence of an individual without participation in a community (a social dimension) and without a relationship to God (a theological dimension) is totally inconceivable. Using modern categories, we would say that the three elements of the lamentation presuppose an understanding in which theology, psychology, and sociology have not yet been separated from each other. (1981: 268)

b. Brueggemann

The implication of Westermann's work is, of course, that contemporary readers of the Psalms (at least within the Christian communities) can lay claim to the same promises and make the same vows. This is an approach that has been considerably developed by Brueggemann, especially in his 'Psalms and the Life of Faith' (1980). He argued that the Psalms can be seen to have a commonality of function in both ancient and modern times, once historically conditioned elements have been set aside, and proposed as a paradigm for interpretation the sequence *orientation–disorientation–reorientation* (1980: 6). It is important to be clear that this is seen as both a hermeneutic for modern readers and a genuine dimension of the 'original' Psalter. He identifies specific representatives of these three types: the first includes songs of creation, wisdom, retribution and blessing; psalms of lament make up the second; and the third includes hymns and songs of thanksgiving. Brueggemann adds to this structure two ideas found in Ricoeur: the hermeneutic of suspicion, and the concept of iconic augmentation. That is, displacement of meaning is necessary for there to be a genuine recovery of interpretation (1980: 10–11). The first of these might be correlated with the idea of disorientation or displacement, the second with reorientation. Finally, the threefold structure can be seen both as a mimesis of life and as a useful way to understand the Psalms and to relate them to life (1980: 13–14). Brueggemann takes his analysis a stage further in a later article in which he seeks to understand the structure of the Psalter as a whole under the rubrics set out above, with Psalms 1; 73; and 150 paradigms of the three elements of his sequence (1990).

Both of these essays in theological interpretation are of interest, and both are bold attempts to win back the Psalms from what might be thought to be an overly historical-critical approach. Nasuti (1998: 42–52) provides a critique of both which is a useful corrective to their approaches. I turn now to my own brief commentary on theological aspects of the Psalms.

4. The Psalms as problem

If there is one thing that the psalmists do well it is complaint. At least a third of the poems can be classed as psalms of lament according to Gunkel's *gattungen*, and they are scattered regularly throughout the Psalter. The percentage falls off dramatically in Books IV and V, in seeming accordance with the widely held belief that the latter part of the Psalter represents the more optimistic liturgy of the second-temple period. Even so, nearly 25 per cent of these 'happy' songs are of the complaining type – the figures are given in Table 6.1 (the list is that of Gillingham (1994: 231)). This seems to suggest at first sight that there was at the heart of the Hebrew experience a considerable sense of disappointment. However, a closer look at the psalms listed below reveals the interesting fact that often the complaint is only voiced in order to provide a pretext for extolling the great mercy or power of God. Thus while Psalm 3 opens with a complaint about the number of foes the psalmist faces (v. 1) and the despairing advice from associates ('many are saying to me, "There is no help for you in God"' v. 2), it quickly segues into a celebration of the security provided by God (vv. 3, 5-6), the assurance of a divine response (v. 4), a triumphalist prayer for the defeat of the enemy (v. 7) and a declaration of deliverance (v. 8). It may in the end be a moot point whether this psalm ought to be classed as a complaint; but even those which dwell at greater length on hardships, such as Psalm 6 (vv. 1-7) frequently turn themselves around in the closing verses (6.8-10). Others (like Psalm 25) dwell more on God's mercy and trustworthiness (vv. 1-10), recognize the probable guilt of the petitioner (v. 11), and end with a complaint – as if to say that, all things considered, the kind of God this is *ought* to be able to resolve the psalmist's problems (vv. 16-22).

Table 6.1 Psalms of Lament

Book I	3, 5, 6, 7, 12, 13, 17, 22, 25, 26, 28, 31, 35, 36, 38, 39, 41	17/41 = 41.5%	
Book II	42, 43, 44, 51, 54, 55, 56, 57, 59, 60, 61, 63, 64, 69, 70, 71	16/31 = 51.5%	42/89 =47%
Book III	74, 77, 79, 80, 82, 83, 85, 86, 88	9/17 = 53%	
Book IV	90, 94, 102, 106	4/17 = 23.5%	15/61 = 24.5%
Book V	108, 109, 120, 123, 126, 130, 137, 140, 141, 142, 143	11/44 = 25%	

A particular plea which is often found is the prayer, 'Rise up, O God!', which may well have associations with the rituals of the ark. It occurs, with variants (the verb is different in 94.2), in 3.7; 7.6; 9.19; 10.12;

12.5; 17.13; 44.26; <u>68.1</u>; 74.22; 94.2; 82.8; 102.13; <u>132.8</u>. All but three of these (9, 68, and 132) are laments. The latter two belong clearly to the liturgy of the ark, and it would be tempting to associate with them Psalm 24 where Yahweh is undoubtedly raised up to enter Jerusalem in triumph, even if the precise words are not used. Psalm 9 is usually combined with Psalm 10 as a single composition, thus bringing it into the general ambit of laments. It is worth noting that Psalm 82 (which may only at a stretch be regarded as a lament) uses mythic language to present a trial in which the other gods are judged and reduced to the level of 'mere mortals'; as such it could well form the climax of a ritual involving the ark.

In short, the belief that the Israelites were prone to almost incessant complaint is very far off the mark. It would be more accurate to say that, as a regular part of both private petition and public liturgy, the frank expression of various kinds of unhappiness was a prelude to, or a consequence of, a robust declaration and defence of the nature of God. Theologically this seems sound: there is little point in clinging to belief in an ineffectual deity or putting one's trust in a god with clay feet (to borrow a metaphor from Daniel). Psychologically, too, it has value: the expression of despair can be part of the healing process, and it is not perhaps too great a stretch of the imagination to substitute for a traditional deity those experiences and relationships which give us hope as humans. The reader is invited to test the truth of these observations by reading through the collected psalms of lament. If nothing else, you will discover the fragility of the whole form-critical approach to the Psalms.

a. Prayers for vengeance

Within the broader compass of the laments in general, there are some specific issues which pose ethical or theological problems. The eagerness with which a number of the psalms urge God to deal violently with enemies, or celebrate the fact that extreme misfortunes have overtaken them, is upsetting to a modern conscience. At least on the personal level we like to believe that we have gone beyond such emotions – though our collective and individual responses to 9/11, the resurgence of both antisemitism and Islamophobia, and the brutalities associated with Abu Ghraib, Guantanamo and Basra, surely warn us that we are not as far removed from (or improved over) the raw feelings of the psalmists as we once fondly believed. The 'we' of this sentiment is, of course, Western; but I do not believe it is less true of humankind as a whole.

A number of these psalms include motivation in the form, usually, of an account of what the enemy/the wicked/the evil-doers did first, thus introducing a kind of tit-for-tat regime. In selecting these psalms I have ignored those which simply seek the disappearance of these people, or justice of an unspecified kind. What remains is a group of verses, spread through the whole Psalter, which makes for depressing, and sometimes quite vivid reading. They are set out in Table 6.2, and those which are also classed as laments are underlined. Perhaps surprisingly, only half turn out to be in that category; surprising also are the further facts that only one is found in Book III, where the loss of the temple is mourned, and that there is a return in popularity of this motif in Book V. Perhaps there are good psychological reasons for these seeming anomalies. At the point when the enemy have done their very worst, there is, I suggest, little point in prayers for vengeance; on the other hand, the more up-beat and eschatological tones of Book V might encourage the belief that (at last) the wicked will receive their just deserts.

Table 6.2 Prayers for specific vengeance
(Psalms of Lament underlined)

Book I	3.7b; 9.5-6; 10.15; 11.6; 17.14; 18.37-42; 21.8-12; 28.3-5; 31.17b-18	9/41 = 22%	
Book II	52.5-7; 55.15, 23; 58.6-9; 63.9-10; 68.2, 21-23; 69.22-28	6/31 = 19%	16/89 =18%
Book III	83.13-17	1/17 = 6%	
Book IV	94.23; 101.1-8	2/17 = 12%	
Book V	109; 110.6; 129.5-8; 137.9; 139.19; 140.10; 141.7; 149.6-9	8/44 = 18%	10/61 = 16%

For those who have the stomach for it, here is a catena of verses from the psalms in Table 6.2, to give a flavour of the mood expressed.

> Deliver me, O my God! For you strike all my enemies on the cheek; you break the teeth of the wicked. Break the arm of the wicked and evildoers! On the wicked he will rain coals of fire and sulphur; a scorching wind shall be the portion of their cup. May their bellies be filled with what you have in store for them; may their children have more than enough; may they leave

something over for their little ones. They cried for help, but there was no one to save them; they cried to the Lord, but he did not answer them. I beat them fine, like dust before the wind; I cast them out like the mire of the streets. Let death come upon them; let them go down alive to Sheol. You, O God, will cast them down into the lowest pit. Let them be like the snail that dissolves into slime; like the untimely birth that never sees the sun. They shall be given over to the power of the sword, they shall be prey for jackals. As smoke is driven away, so drive them away; as wax melts before the fire, let the wicked perish before God. I will bring them back from the depths of the sea, so that you may bathe your feet in blood, so that the tongues of your dogs may have their share from the foe. He will execute judgement among the nations, filling them with corpses; he will shatter heads over the wide earth. Happy shall they be who take your little ones and dash them against the rock! Let burning coals fall on them! Let them be flung into pits, no more to rise! Like a rock that one breaks apart and shatters on the land, so shall their bones be strewn at the mouth of Sheol.

And, as a coda, in almost the last psalm of the collection (149.6-7) the worshippers are exhorted in the following terms

Let the high praises of God be in their throats
    and two-edged swords in their hands,
to execute vengeance on the nations
    and punishment on the peoples.

These grim prayers (or more optimistically, fantasies) are not peripheral to the Psalter. They speak of a kind of theology which is, to say the least, robust. They speak, dare I say, more truly to our own emotions (at times) than we would like to admit. They are, we must hope, primitive, coming from 'another country' where 'they do things differently' (to mangle somewhat the opening sentence of L.P. Hartley's *The Go-between*). But how should the interpreter or singer of the Psalms deal with them?

One honourable tradition sees them as having cathartic or preventive effect. By voicing these unacceptable sentiments we remove a potential trauma, the kind of wound that festers hidden when we do not fully confront our feelings about those who have harmed us. We offer our worst desires to God (or on the psychiatrist's couch) and by so doing divert them into safe hands.

There is, however, a risk in allowing these loaded texts the oxygen of publicity (as Margaret Thatcher once notoriously said of quite a different perceived danger). It is that the mark of biblical or ecclesiastical authority might – for some – sanction a literal reading.

It is not so long ago in European history that Christians were slaughtering each other in the name of their own particular version of the truth. It seems more than likely that the Psalms played a part in this grim business. Prothero (1914: 222, 244) provides a couple of test cases. In the first, summing up the Huguenot period, he remarks that it was not only their virtues that

> the Psalms had fostered. From the same book they justified their ferocity. To them Rome was Babylon and the Reformed Church was Sion. Their enemies were God's enemies. They were his appointed instruments of vengeance, and they made war in the spirit of Calvin's commentary on Psalms cxxxvii., verses 8, 9, and of his defence of its imprecations on the women and children of their foes.

The second reference is to Cromwell, of whom Prothero writes:

> Throughout the war he never ceases to speak the language of the Psalms. He relies not on men and visible helps ... . It is God's cause in which he fights. In God is his strength. It is God who says, 'Up and be doing, and I will stand by you and help you.' It is God who makes the Royalists as 'stubble' (Ps. lxxxiii., verse 13) before the swords of the Puritans. In him and in his troopers burns the spirit of young Walton, who died at Marston Moor with one thing only lying heavy on his soul – that 'God had not suffered him to be any more the executioner of His enemies.'

The power of such religious texts to influence the actions of certain people is indisputable: we cannot censor them, nor can we neutralize their force. I conclude, therefore, that it is essential that they remain in the mainstream discourse (for good or ill) so that at the very least the range of available interpretations is kept available. The Bible is a dangerous book: those who want to explore that danger further might be interested to read *Sanctified Aggression* (Bekkenkamp and Sherwood 2003) which explores some of these issues more generally.

b. Unmerited suffering

A second problem lies in the perception (entirely accurate) that much suffering and hardship are in the main unmerited. This is a conundrum which is at least as old as the first human society which decided there was some kind of vaguely benevolent (or rational!) deity in charge. No-one living in the century after the Holocaust and its imitators in Cambodia, Rwanda, Darfur, and who knows where else, needs reminding that the God of love who takes an interest in us and has some rudimentary sense of justice, has been served notice by a considerable body of his or her former supporters. Perhaps this is a little flippant – but sometimes we need the starkness of a colloquial approach to let us cut through the obscurities that theology sometimes throws over issues. And if there is one thing we can affirm about the psalmists, it is that they cut to the quick, and rarely minced their words. It is, and remains, a striking paradox that they nevertheless continued to produce some of the most magnificent hymns of praise the world possesses. Perhaps there is a clue here.

The Psalms, admittedly, lack the sheer anguish of Job; nothing matches his terrible prayer in Job 3 that it would be better had he never been born. A closer parallel is found in those personal prayers in Jeremiah which are often referred to as the 'confessions of Jeremiah'. These are a series of short poems which give expression to the poet's sense of being a victim. In order to emphasize the psalms-quality of these pieces I have noted only the core complaint in each case, leaving out elements of a more prophetic kind which are often included. The list is: Jer. 11.18-20; 12.1-4; 15.15-18; 17.14-18; 18.19-23; 20.7-13; and 20.14-18 (the precise delineation is my own). Most are readily recognizable from the psalms provided in Table 6.1; Jer. 20.14-15 is perhaps best considered as the expression of a similar sentiment to that of Job:

> Cursed be the day
>   on which I was born!
> The day when my mother bore me,
>   let it not be blessed!
> Cursed be the man
>   who brought the news to my father, saying,
> 'A child is born to you, a son',
>   making him very glad.

One of the best overviews of these intriguing compositions is still Robert Carroll's in *From Chaos to Covenant* (1981: 107–30). Carroll rejects the popular view of these pieces as 'paradigms of personal religion based on prophecy' (1981: 107), noting on the contrary, in respect of motifs found in the 'confessions', that they are so common in the Psalms 'that we see in their occurrence in the Jeremiah tradition the strong influence of liturgical language from cultic sources' (1981: 109); and further, that 'The strong resemblances between the language of the complaints [of Jeremiah] and the lament psalms in the Psalter increase the likelihood that the editors of the tradition were intent on presenting Jeremiah as an intercessor for the nation' (1981: 114).

He goes on to observe that

> there is a double sense of reference and application to the prophet and the community. This interpenetration of the individual and the collective is very characteristic of the way the Psalms work, and illustrates the common bond between the reflection upon and expression of experience in the Psalms and in the Jeremiah tradition. (1981: 123)

Carroll concludes that, '[a]s in the Psalms, the resolution of the complainant's problem is the presence of Yahweh' (1981: 128).

The claims to innocence made in the Psalms themselves take different forms. Words similar to the rhetoric in Job 31 are found in Ps. 7.3-5: 'O Lord my God, if I have done this, if there is wrong in my hands ... then let the enemy pursue and overtake me', which clearly expects the answer, 'No, of course you have not done any wrong!' Incidentally, this is reminiscent of the encounter between Jesus and Zacchaeus in Lk. 19.1-9, where the popular assumption that Zacchaeus was a 'bad man' redeemed by his encounter with Jesus is belied by precisely the same literary convention (Lk. 19.5): 'Zacchaeus stood there and said to the Lord, "Look, half of my possessions, Lord, I will give to the poor; and *if* [my emphasis] I have defrauded anyone of anything, I will pay back four times as much."' These are not, in fact, the words of a guilty man; and in the story it is only the bystanders who so judge him. His only 'faults' were being vertically challenged and being a tax officer, neither (despite popular prejudice) entailing moral turpitude!

Psalm 26 makes a more straightforward case for integrity and purity – perhaps at a slightly sanctimonious level (vv. 4-7). Here the plea is prophylactic: because I am virtuous, O Lord, protect me from possible calamity (see also 86.2-7). In 44.17-22 there is a combination of this motif with that in Psalm 7 ('We have not forgotten you ...'; 'If we had forgotten the name of our God ...'), challenging God to waken up and come to their help (vv. 23-26). In other places (e.g. 59.3-4; 73.13-14) the poet complains that being innocent and virtuous is of no avail: the reward for goodness is to be plagued and punished! But overall it is surprising how rarely the direct claim to innocence is made. The sufferings of the psalmists are frequently described, and the impression is given that they are a consequence of the oppression of enemies, whether human or cosmic, but one that seems almost to be an unavoidable part of the identity of the true Israelite. I am reminded a little of the 'persecution convention' that accompanies certain kinds of religious enthusiasm: true faith requires an experience of oppression, and so the rhetoric comes to play a part in the religious identity of many whose physical circumstances seem far from uncomfortable. It is as if all prophets have to be rejected in order to authenticate their calling, and all poets have to live in penury lest their muse be thought to be false. We have journeyed some way from the impassioned plea of the genuinely oppressed to the danger that this motif may come to be little more than a religious fashion. I cannot judge (nor would I wish to) the validity of the persecution so often described in the Psalms; but I believe it is important for contemporary readers to be cautious about any claim to identify with these feelings.

Finally, in this section, we should note that just as innocence is from time to time protested, so is guilt on occasion accepted. Sometimes it is safely in the past – 'Do not remember the sins of my youth' (25.7), though the same psalm (in v. 18) admits continuing guilt: 'forgive all my sins'. The active confession of sin and a plea for forgiveness is graphically enunciated in 32.5 (cf. 38.3-4, 18; 41.4):

> Then I acknowledged my sin to you,
>   and I did not hide my iniquity;
> I said, 'I will confess my transgressions to the Lord',
>   and you forgave the guilt of my sin.

Perhaps the best known and most dramatic of these confessions is in Ps. 51.1-5, famously (though almost certainly erroneously) associated with David's heinous behaviour in relation to Bathsheba. It is worth setting these words out in full, because the rhetorical flourish with which they end has sometimes been used in support of such influential doctrines as the belief in 'original' sin; arguably Augustine's most baleful gift to the western church, both Catholic and Protestant:

> Have mercy on me, O God,
>   according to your steadfast love;
> according to your abundant mercy
>   blot out my transgressions.
> Wash me thoroughly from my iniquity,
>   and cleanse me from my sin.
> For I know my transgressions,
>   and my sin is ever before me.
> Against you, you alone, have I sinned,
>   and done what is evil in your sight,
> so that you are justified in your sentence

and blameless when you pass judgement.
Indeed, I was born guilty,
a sinner when my mother conceived me.

The sense of a personal confession of failure is strong here; but also a curious mismatch: for if this were to be in any sense relevant to David, one would have expected an expression of regret directed towards the *people* he had harmed. Instead we find that it is *God* who is the only aggrieved party. This might be conventional; but it does reflect a problem in Christian tradition, though perhaps not Jewish, that the guilty can be absolved by someone other than the person against whom they have offended.

The sinfulness of the nation as a whole is admitted in Pss. 78.17, 32 and 106.6, as part of a Deuteronomistically influenced theology of national guilt and consequent punishment, perhaps contrasted with statements like that of Ps. 85.1-3, where national forgiveness and restoration is given to Jacob. The same idea, expressed in personal terms, is to be found in Ps. 103.10: 'He does not deal with us according to our sins, nor repay us according to our iniquities' – a verse followed immediately by a form of the famous benediction most fully enunciated in Exod. 34.6-7:

The Lord, the Lord
a God merciful and gracious,
slow to anger,
and abounding in steadfast love and faithfulness,
keeping steadfast love for the thousandth generation,
forgiving iniquity and transgression and sin,
yet by no means clearing the guilty,
but visiting the iniquity of the parents
upon the children
and the children's children
to the third and the fourth generation.

The precise meaning of this paradoxical proclamation is not entirely clear; but it does seem to imply that guilt must be borne, though iniquity will be forgiven. It is tempting to see this as an expression of a psychological and theological truth: that 'cheap' forgiveness without repentance or the effort to make reparation is worthless. Phyllis Trible (1978) has explored this text as it journeys through the Old Testament in a book which is well worth reading.

c. The hiddenness of God

The third specific awkwardness I want to note is that of the hiddenness of God. It is interesting that one of the major religious responses to the Holocaust, that of Eliezer Berkovits, uses precisely this device to provide one possible account of the Shoah. Steven Katz (1983: 268–86 (270–71)) explains Berkovits's position succinctly:

> Taking his cue from the biblical doctrine of *hester panim* ('the Hiding Face of God'), Berkovits claims that God's hiddenness is required for man to be a moral creature. God's hiddenness brings into being the possibility for ethically valent human action, for by 'absenting' Himself from history He creates the reality of human freedom which is necessary for moral behaviour. For human good and evil to be real possibilities God has to respect the decisions of mankind and be bound by them. Among the necessary corollaries of this ethical autonomy is that God has to abstain from reacting immediately to immoral deeds, and certainly from acting in advance to suppress them. But it is just here that the fundamental paradox emerges: for a moral humanity to exist freedom must exist, yet it is the nature of freedom that it is always open to the possibility of abuse.
>
> The corollary of this, as Berkovits understands the situation, is that 'while He [God] shows forbearance with the wicked, He must turn a deaf ear to the anguished cries of the violated'.

In a good many psalms God is chided for 'hiding himself', or implored not to do so – an apparently naive understanding which nevertheless has some quite sophisticated implications, as we have seen in relation to the Holocaust. It is an idea that can be seen in different ways: on the one hand, as a sign that the benevolent parent has (apparently wilfully) withdrawn for their own unfathomable purposes; but on the other, as a test of human moral and ethical probity. For if we are creatures of free will (as many religions claim) it is necessary for us to demonstrate that freedom in difficult circumstances, to be, as it were, grown-up and godlike. The only way in which that freedom can be genuinely tested is if God not only withdraws, but also refrains from baling us out when the consequences of our weakness or ethical failure become all too apparent.

In the Psalms, of course, it is the former sense that is more common. Thus Ps. 13.1, 'How long, O Lord? Will you forget me for ever? How long will you hide your face from me?' (cf. 29.9; 30.7; 44.24; 69.17; 88.14; 89.46; 102.2; 143.7). Once it is the wicked who believes (erroneously) that God is in hiding and therefore will not see his wrongdoing (10.11), and once the psalmist pleads with God to 'hide his face' from the poet's sin (51.9). But it would be fair to say that, for the Psalter, God's hiddenness is simply bad, something without constructive features. There are, elsewhere in the Old Testament, alternative voices which can be read constructively alongside this rather limited perspective to provide a reading somewhat closer to that of our second possibility. I refer on the one hand to the Torah concept that God's face is of necessity hidden because no human being can bear to look upon it, and on the other to Qoheleth's somewhat bleak conclusion that for the most part we are on our own. The former is given as a direct injunction to Moses in Exod. 33.20: 'You cannot see my face, for no-one shall see me and live', which is alluded to in the stories of Hagar (Gen. 16.13), Jacob at Peniel (Gen. 32.20), the elders with Moses on the mountain top (Exod. 24.11) and Manoah, Samson's father (Judg. 6.22). Both Moses (Exod. 3.6) and Isaiah (Isa. 6.5) express the same fear of seeing God. For Qoheleth, on the other hand, the question of seeing God is not even on the horizon: God no doubt exists, but at a remote distance and inscrutable in manner. The effect is that we are morally on our own. Whether either the Torah or Qoheleth is in any way expanding upon the thinking of the Psalms may be doubted, but intertextually the combination of the two suggests a theological development going beyond the more naive starting point. Incidentally, it is clear from the distribution of these references that this notion is not limited to any particular period of the Psalter's development.

5. Positive themes in the Psalms

William P. Brown (2002) makes a strong case for the importance of the use of metaphor in the Psalms as a means of conveying/signifying meaning to the reader. His *Seeing the Psalms* is a striking contribution to the theological and poetic interpretation of the Psalms. While making explicit his own position within the Christian tradition (something which seems to be a predominant feature of theology of the Psalter: thus Westermann, Kraus and Brueggemann), he nonetheless maintains a generosity of interpretation which opens out the religious, poetic and mythic diversity of the Psalms in a helpful way. Brown opens with a methodological chapter in which he explores the poetics of metaphor, and stresses the central role of metaphor as an effective means to both understanding and appreciating the poetry in which it is used; he then devotes two chapters to key motifs in the Psalter: the concepts of *refuge* and *the pathway*. Four central chapters deal with four physical representations; respectively, the tree (Psalm 1), the sun

(Psalm 19), water (Psalm 42) and the animal kingdom (Psalm 104). In each case he relates the images to matters of belief and practice, and illustrates them by means of found objects from the ancient Near East – making use, among others, of the work of Othmar Keel (1978). While I will be able to offer a few pointers here, readers are recommended to look at Brown's book for a much more extensive and informative treatment of the subject. A similar approach, but with a different emphasis, is taken by Alexander Ryrie (2004). In his *Deliver Us from Evil: Reading the Psalms as Poetry*, Ryrie focuses on images of stress and deliverance; thus his work is more precisely directed to the particular theological problem of theodicy than Brown's more wide-ranging study.

a. History and myth

A question worth raising at the outset here is whether, in the ancient world, history and myth were distinct categories. I do not want to embark on a lengthy discussion at this point of topics which have often been reviewed. But it would be irresponsible to ignore the problem when we are attempting to explore the theological importance of these phenomena as they appear in the Psalms. It is certainly true to say that what counts as historical evidence in modern terminology was largely unknown to the ancient world: largely, but not entirely. The concept of written evidence was available, as is seen in the well-known cross-references in the Old Testament to such sources as 'The Book of the Annals of the Kings of Israel' (2 Kgs 1.18). Indirect evidence of the use of written sources is seen in the extent to which scripture quotes itself – most obviously from our perspective, in the repetition of parts of psalms (as we noted in Chapter 3, Ps. 144.1-7 seems to be a patchwork of phrases from other psalms, as does Psalm 86; Psalms 57 and 60 quote extensively from Psalm 108; and Psalm 70 is a repetition of Ps. 40.13-17). And if we were in doubt as to the existence of a meaningful concept of the past, we would only need to look at the book of Deuteronomy which is cast entirely as a reminder of past events. What is obviously different is the lack of a critical perspective on supposed evidence from the past on the one hand, and the apparent readiness to accept improbable (to a modern ear) content as straight fact. This is why, for example, the 'historicity' of the exodus from Egypt is such a vexed question. To ancient readers the question seems not to have arisen, not least because miraculous events attributed to God were a regular aspect of the narrative of the past; a position now almost impossible to imagine within the academic study of history.

Myths are characterized by the bringing to centre stage of those elements of the miraculous and of divine intervention which are somewhat incidental to history. Indeed, they are in an important sense *about* God: the divine being is the principal character, rather than one who acts on behalf of others. They are, then, history if we can understand history as 'narratives about God's past'. The language used to describe them is similar to that used of human participants. God speaks, acts, strikes, attacks, defeats, shapes, walks, orders and commands just as powerful human figures do. There are good grounds, therefore, for believing that the psalmists and their readers would not have made the kind of categorical distinction modern readers make between these genres. Moreover, the fact that either myth (74.12-17) or history – albeit of a metaphorical kind (80.8-11) – can constitute the review of God's past action which forms the pivotal point in psalms of lament suggests a minimal distinction between the two.

Despite these observations, when we look more closely at the distribution of these two types of material in the Psalter, a surprising distinction emerges. Without wishing to claim an exhaustive or systematic listing of psalms which display overtly mythic or historical features, Table 6.3 provides a reasonably comprehensive overview of these types of psalms, and their distribution in the five books.

Table 6.3 Myth and history in the Psalms

	Myth	History
Book I	18.7-15; 29.3-9; 33.6-7	
Book II	46; 65	68.7-23
Book III	74.12-17; 77.16-20; 89.9-12	77.11-15; 78; 80.8-11; 81; 83.9-12
Book IV		105; 106
Book V	114; 136.4-9	107; 135.8-12; 136.10-22

It turns out that there are ten in the category of myth (I have identified two – 77 and 136 – as belonging to both), of which eight (80%) are in Books I–III; on the other hand, of the twelve which I have identified as historical, eleven (92%) are in Books III–V. This may reflect a change which might be correlated with a post-exilic preference for *heilsgeschichte* (sacred history), with more overtly mythic language finding less favour. The numbers, however, are small, and should not be interpreted as representing an abandonment of mythic language, merely a change of emphasis. The major overlap is in Book III, which may not be surprising given (a) that no fewer than nine laments are to be found among its seventeen members, and (b) that this book marks a crucial period (in my view, the exile) during which recent events were being assimilated and a previously unthinkable future contemplated.

When we examine the historical psalms more closely, some interesting nuances emerge. The first of the great 'historical review' psalms is 78; all of the others are in the last two books. Three (105–07) straddle Books IV and V, while the last (136) seems to have more of the character of a historical litany, with its constant repetition of the refrain 'for his steadfast love endures for ever'. All of the other historical segments which I have identified deal with the exodus and the conquest (68 and 135, both; 77, 80 and 81, exodus alone; 83 conquest alone), indicating a rather clear focus. When we add to this the fact that 105, though it begins with the patriarchal period, concludes with the occupation of the 'promised land'; 106 – in a more negative mode – dwells mostly on the sins of the people during the period of the wilderness wandering; and 136 also focuses on the exodus and the wilderness, we see that for the liturgical and poetic tradition 'history' means (almost exclusively) the exodus, wilderness and conquest tradition. The only exception, and the one which could be argued to have a Deuteronomistic approach to the broader historical tradition, is 78. Brueggemann, in *Abiding Astonishment* (1991), reflects on the importance of the four great historical psalms (78, 105, 106 and 136) and argues that they 'create, evoke, suggest, and propose a network of symbols, metaphors, images, memories and hopes so that "the world," in each successive generation, is perceived, experienced and practiced in a specific way' (1991: 21). He identifies this 'world' as 'intergenerational, covenantly shaped, morally serious, dialogically open, and politically demanding'. This is a short book, little more than an article in length, and Brueggemann may, to some readers, seem guilty of essentializing or specially privileging Israelite history to theological ends. But his reading is, if nothing else, a pointer to the fact that these psalms are far more than sources of comparative history (if indeed they are that at all).

The psalms which have a more clearly mythological aspect are much less coherent in theme. A number do clearly reflect aspects of the exodus legend, in a mythologized form: thus 74.12-17; 77.16-20; and 114. Others dramatize creation (33.6-7; 136.4-9) or the battle against the primordial waters and other natural forces (18.7-15; 29.3-9; 74.12-17; 89.9-12), with echoes in the second group of the mythic language associated with Baal and Hadad. Given that the language of the exodus myth is strongly influenced by that of the battle with the unruly forces of the sea, it is reasonable to conclude that even the mythological psalms are bound up to a considerable, though not exclusive, extent with the same complex of traditions as those of a more historical character. One psalm – 46 – remains somewhat outside the regular pattern. It does have aspects of the battle against the forces of nature, but adds an interesting dimension (picked up much later in Rev. 22.1-5): that of the city of God blessed by a mystical river.

Without wanting to force the evidence, it therefore seems to me that there is a strong tendency towards an interpretive focus on the historical narratives of the books of Exodus and Numbers, reinforced by the redeployment of mythic language in the service – to a very considerable extent – of the same complex of traditions. In other words, what we know from other sources in the Old Testament is reinforced in the Psalter: one of the dominant poetic traditions of Israel is the grand myth/legend/history of the Exodus. This is not, of course, the only important thematic emphasis to be discerned in the Psalms, but it is an important one, and identifying it as we have done is a significant contribution to the theological interpretation of the poetry of Israel.

b. Messianic notes

We have had occasion already to note the importance of the messianic theme in the Qumran Psalms. The topic is in some ways a difficult one to broach, on account of its dominant Christian aspects, and the reticence with which Jewish tradition has handled the subject. Centuries of suffering the accusation of having rejected 'the messiah' whenever it suited Christendom to use that charge have led, understandably, to a downplaying of messianic hopes within the period from 200 BCE to 200 CE when rabbinic Judaism was emerging. We now know that it was undoubtedly an important strand in the biblical tradition, albeit a dangerous one (as the number of failed messiahs makes clear – of whose number, from a Jewish perspective, Jesus is certainly one). It was a significant causal factor in the two Jewish wars against the Romans, and was seductive enough to win the support of Rabbi Akiva in 130 CE, when he endorsed the claims of Bar Kochba to be the messiah. This *nachleben* (afterlife) of the hope of a messianic saviour should not, however, blind us to the reality of its importance in the Old Testament in general, and the Psalms in particular.

The signs that a psalm might be read (or have been intended to be read) in this way are fairly straightforward. A maximal position would start from the inverse of that taken by John Eaton in his study of royal psalms (see above, Chapter 3): namely, any psalm which is overtly royal is potentially messianic. Thus we might begin with Gunkel's set of royal psalms (2; 18; 20; 21; 45; 72; 101; 110; 132; 144.1-11), tacitly supported by the likelihood that the enthusiasm the Chronicler shows for David and Solomon is at least in part an early manifestation of that idealization of the Davidic dynasty which is at the heart of messianic theology. To those we might add other instances of key vocabulary (the anointed, the horn that sprouts, the crown that shines, son of God).

Psalm 2 is, I believe, undoubtedly messianic (Hunter 1999: 110–13). The fourfold designation of the king ('his anointed', 'my king', 'my son' and 'kiss the son' (aramaic *bar*) – this is the literal meaning of the Hebrew of v. 12) combined with the triumphalist language of the psalm constitute a compelling case. Psalms 18 and 20 are more difficult, and I shall return to them later. When we turn to Psalm 21 we find ourselves immersed in the language, apparently, of a powerful ruling monarch, but language which it only takes a small shift in perspective to see as messianic. From the perspective, that is, of the same period when the Qumran group was shaping its views of David, we read of a king to whom is given: a crown of gold; length of days for ever and ever; glory; splendour and majesty; and blessings. Moreover (vv. 8-12) he will enjoy comprehensive victory over all his enemies, in partnership (v. 9b) with Yahweh. It is a pity that the technical term 'anointed' is not used in this psalm, for in all other respects it is a model of the military messianic redeemer of Israel.

Psalm 45 is often characterized as an *epithalamion* – an elaborate piece composed to celebrate the king's wedding. Once again, even if this were its original function, the case for a messianic reading is strong. The sheer density of allusion in vv. 4-8a surely speaks for itself:

> In your majesty ride on victoriously
>> for the cause of truth and to defend the right;
>> let your right hand teach you dread deeds.
> Your arrows are sharp
>> in the heart of the king's enemies;
>> the peoples fall under you.
> Your throne, O God, endures for ever and ever.
>> Your royal sceptre is a sceptre of equity;
>> you love righteousness and hate wickedness.

Therefore God, your God, has anointed you
>with the oil of gladness beyond your companions;
>your robes are all fragrant with myrrh and aloes and cassia.

The theme of comprehensive triumph over enemies is to the fore, but
note also his defence of 'the right' and his love of 'righteousness'; the
phrase 'Your throne, O God', which is tantamount to identifying
the human subject of the psalm with God; his 'sceptre of equity';
and his having been anointed. And here there is a further significant
touch: the reference to 'oil of gladness' and to the fragrances in the
king's robes hints at a further role – that of the priest. Compare the
elaborate recipe for the anointing oil in Exod. 30.22-33, especially
the last verse: 'Whoever compounds any like it or whoever puts any
of it on an unqualified person shall be cut off from the people'; the
same recipe is used to describe wisdom's presence in the sanctuary
in Sir. 24.15. In this connection it is appropriate also to anticipate
the curious language of Ps. 110.4 'a priest for ever after the order of
Melchizedek' and the graphic image in Ps. 133.2 (which follows hot
on the heels of 132, another messianic psalm):

It [unity] is like the precious oil on the head,
>running down upon the beard,
on the beard of Aaron,
>running down over the collar of his robes.

In short, there is compelling evidence for a reading of these verses in
the context of a very high understanding of the messiah, combining
divine, priestly and military roles. But that is not all; for Psalm 45 is
undoubtedly the celebration of a wedding which concludes with the
anticipation of descendants (v. 16):

In the place of ancestors, you, O king, shall have sons;
>you will make them princes in all the earth.

The role of the messiah is so often construed as being that of a
supernatural being who brings closure to this present order that we
forget that in its earliest formulations it referred to the coming of
God's ideal king; and a king, of course, implies a dynasty – one that in
this case would be expected to introduce a permanently benign rule.
It is in this expectation, for example, that Ps. 132.11-12 writes:

The Lord swore to David a sure oath
>from which he will not turn back:

'One of the sons of your body
  I will set on your throne.
If your sons keep my covenant
  and my decrees that I shall teach them,
their sons also, for evermore
  shall sit on your throne.'

I will not speculate here on the identity of the king's bride; perhaps it only acquires hermeneutical significance in later Jewish and Christian tradition, just as does the Song of Songs, where respectively Torah and the Church might be understood to fill that role.

The next royal psalm, 72, is entitled 'A Psalm of Solomon', an attribution only found once again, in Psalm 127. It concludes Book III, and is one of the key royal psalms in Wilson's analysis of the redaction of the Psalter. Whatever its relationship to the historical king Solomon (faint, at best, in my assessment), at its heart is the celebration of a mystical ruler who has supernatural powers to deliver justice, prosperity and deliverance, to provide for a fertile and productive land, to (as usual) rule 'from sea to sea, and from the River to the ends of the earth' and humiliate his enemies, and to be expected to live 'while the sun endures, and as long as the moon' that his name may 'endure for ever, his fame continue as long as the sun'. The final two verses give the game away, as it were, in that their address to Yahweh makes it clear that all these wonders are in God's gift alone. Thus the marvellous king whom the psalm has so fulsomely celebrated can be none other than Yahweh's king. The term 'anointed' is not used in Psalm 72, but in all other respects it falls clearly into the category of a messianic psalm.

Psalm 101 is one of the most problematic of the royal psalms to explain, not least because the designation of it as being royal is at least in part a last-resort effort to make sense of its subject. For though it begins with a rather typical personal hymn of praise and commitment (vv. 1-4), it then segues into a condemnation, from the perspective of someone in authority, of those who do wrong, together with the promise of a reward for those who are faithful. The only officials who might have such power are, before 587, the king and, later under the restored theocracy, the high priest. The sins identified and the reference to 'my house' in vv. 5-7 are much more reminiscent of the criteria imposed on pilgrims in the entrance liturgies in Psalms 15 and 24 than they are of royal prerogatives:

One who secretly slanders a neighbour
  I will destroy.

A haughty look and an arrogant heart
    I will not tolerate.
I will look with favour on the faithful in the land,
    so that they may live with me;
whoever walks in the way that is blameless
    shall minister to me.
No one who practises deceit
    shall remain in my house;
no one who utters lies
    shall continue in my presence.

It is not easy to resolve this dilemma. The simplest (though least plausible) solution would be to discern a different voice – perhaps that of God – speaking from v. 5 to v. 7, with the psalm concluding with a vow paid by the psalmist to work to eradicate evildoers from the land. Unfortunately there is nothing in the language to support this division, and the fact that 'my house' (here meaning either *temple* or *palace*) is found both in v. 2 and in v. 7 points to the opposite conclusion. A variation of this option, which avoids the problem of the repeated reference to 'my house', might be to regard vv. 1-2a as the psalmist's introduction, with the rest on the lips of the authority figure. There are grammatical grounds for this: the opening three verbs of the psalm have a specific grammatical form (the cohortative) which is not repeated in the rest of the poem, and which are best translated as 'let me ...'. The opening of the psalm would then become:

Let me sing of loyalty and of justice;
    to you, O Lord, let me sing.
Let me study the way that is blameless.
    When shall I attain it?

What follows is then in the present tense, representing the character of the one who is answering the psalmist's plea: 'I walk with integrity of heart with my house', and so on. And who is this respondent? I believe that the best reading suggests an exalted priestly figure, perhaps indicative of that other strand in the messiah which is certainly found in the writings from Qumran, and which is perhaps suggested by Ps. 110.4, 'A priest for ever, according to the order of Melchizedek'. There is one further clue to be noted: the verb behind the phrase 'shall minister to me' in v. 6 is a root (*sharat*) which is almost exclusively used of the service of God. Of its 76 occurrences, 65 clearly refer to this usage, one is in Psalm 101, and the remaining ten constitute a few scattered references to the service of kings or prophets. Furthermore, both occurrences of the noun *service* are of a cultic kind. Within the context of the Psalms, and in the absence of any clear indication of a royal provenance (*pace* Gunkel and most commentaries), this is the obvious meaning of this term here: the religious service of Yahweh or at least of the temple. I conclude, therefore, that in Psalm 101 we may be justified in identifying a priestly divine figure which may well have been recognizable within the messianic terminology of the Maccabean and Qumran traditions. It is curious that there are no identifiable references to Psalm 101 in the New Testament. Neither Moyise and Menken in their comprehensive study of Psalms in the NT (2004) nor Shires (1974) offer a single instance, and the cross-reference NRSV (Manser 2003) provides only two very vague and secondary allusions (2a: Mt. 5.48; 7d: Rev. 22.15). Given the prominent use of Psalm 110, which also has a priestly focus, and the importance of Psalm 101 to 11QPs[a] (on this see Flint (1997: 194-98)), where it is significantly tied to Psalm 110, there is something of a mystery here.

There is no such mystery in connection with our next two royal psalms, 110 and 132. The former, while undoubtedly complex and in places obscure, can hardly be doubted as a royal messianic psalm. It was clearly identified as such in the New Testament: it is one of the most frequently cited, and forms an important part of the argument in Hebrews about Jesus's priestly nature. Whether or not 'Melchizedek' is a misreading of the phrase 'righteous king' hardly matters, since it is the priestly character of the messianic king which is plainly advocated. I have commented on this elsewhere (Hunter 2004: 85–87) in an essay on the mysterious figure of Melchizedek. Psalm 132 is equally unequivocally a messianic composition, as the concluding verses make clear:

> There I will cause a horn to sprout up for David;
>> I have prepared a lamp for my anointed one.
> His enemies I will clothe with disgrace,
>> but on him, his crown will gleam.

Note also the parallel 'David' and 'your anointed one' in v. 10, and see further my more detailed exegesis (Hunter 1999: 221–5); though, like Psalm 101, its profile in the New Testament is scarcely visible.

Gunkel's final candidate was Ps. 144.1-11, the decision to divide the psalm being taken presumably on the basis of a change of speaker from 'I' to 'we' in v. 12. Anderson (1972: II, 931) notes that the 'first part is largely a mosaic of various fragments of other psalms, especially Ps. 18', a view shared by most commentators. However, they also for the most part share the view that this has to be a post-exilic composition, which makes the royal context rather problematic at first sight. Given the probable lateness of this piece, it is hard to see how it can be other than some kind of messianic composition – one which emphasizes the 'warrior king' aspect, and looks forward to the kind of prosperity which the messianic age will bring. It is, therefore, a human (if naive) expression of the hope of a better future. And the fact that it makes emphatic use of Psalm 18 opens the door to an interesting possibility: that the latter psalm, which we left to one side at an earlier stage, was itself seen in messianic terms in the later post-exilic period. What is of particular interest in making this connection is the possibility that the messiah might be subject to real human weakness, to require the intervention of God to keep him safe from the threat of the primeval waters (vv. 1-2, 7, 10). By way of contrast, the use of the 'what is man?' motif in vv. 3-4, which reverses the positive use of the same theme in Ps. 8.4, might suggest that the ideal king is superior to or above mere transitory mortals (note the use of 'them' and 'they' rather than 'us' and 'we'). I suggest, therefore, that it is a hypothesis worth considering that Psalms 18 and 20, whatever their original *Sitz-im-Leben*, have become by association messianic psalms in which the emphasis is on the humanity of the royal redeemer. The last verse of Psalm 18 is surely significant in the light of what we have said so far:

> Great triumphs he gives to his king,
>> and shows steadfast love to his anointed,
>> to David and his descendants for ever.

It is tempting at this point to turn to Isaiah 53, as indeed early Christianity did in its attempt to explain a crucified messiah; but that may be a turn too far in what is, after all, only a summary review.

c. Piety and personal prayer

Many years ago, Christoph Barth (1961 [1966]) suggested a thematic approach to the Psalms in which he identified a number of topics which are of lasting significance. They are:

(a) The righteous sinner. The Psalms convey a clear sense of humanity's lowliness; but equally a strong feeling of outraged innocence. This paradox is perhaps explained by seeing that righteousness is what the worshipper achieves through worship. Thus to confess one's guilt is also the action of a righteous person; for, knowing that we require the conferring of righteousness through worship, we do not (like the ungodly) refuse to confess our guilt.

(b)   The wicked enemy. They are mentioned very frequently, and feature in the most 'offensive' passages. They can hardly be identified as historical enemies: the descriptions are formal and stylized; these enemies are 'forces of the ungodly', perhaps mythic, perhaps partisan.

(c)   The power of death and its defeat. Death in the Psalms is almost personified, a tangible enemy, perhaps rooted in the Canaanite god Mot.

(d)   The fundamentals of faith. God is a person, known to be dependable because of interventions in the history of Israel. These actions are of a special character, belonging to the 'history of salvation' (Heilsgeschichte), and are limited in number: Egypt, exodus, the Red Sea, wilderness, Sinai, entry into the land, David, and the supernatural acts of God the creator.

(1961 [1966]: 39-61)

In a sense, what this implies is that further hermeneutical moves away from the original purpose of the Psalms are legitimate for communities of faith (be they Jewish, Christian or whatever). Biblical-critical interpretation is only the base-line. Of course it should not be ignored; and we do not have carte blanche to return to a naive christological or individualistic hermeneutic. But we can seek legitimate ways to reapply these ancient hymns to contemporary life and worship, bringing to this reappraisal the insights won from a century and a half of critical endeavour.

A recent study by H.N. Wallace (2005), *Words to God, Word from God : the Psalms in the Prayer and Preaching of the Church*, takes up specifically the use of the Psalms in the prayer, preaching and worship of the Church, examining its history and the application of particular psalms in this direction. Barth spelled this out in particular in his understanding of the Psalter as a school of prayer (1966: 36-9):

(1)   Prayer is always and fundamentally praise.
(2)   A sign of true prayer is humility, it comes 'out of the depths', but is not ultimately pessimistic: its concern is not with distress as such, but with taking that distress to God.
(3)   Even that which reveals our baser nature can and should be spoken of in prayer. (Cf. vengeance prayers and prayers of complaint.)
(4)   Prayer is communal, even when it is done in solitude. The 'I' of prayer is always the 'I' of the community, not the 'Ego' of the individual.

(5)   Specific intercession and petition is almost wholly absent.

This last point may be worthy of some attention. One of the Hasidim gives this advice: 'If you see a fire-engine rushing by in the direction of your residence, you must not pray that your house is not on fire. For if your house is on fire, your prayer is impossible of fulfilment; and if your house is not on fire, you are in effect praying that your neighbour's house is burning.' In other words, don't pray for sun at the Sunday School Picnic: the farmer may prefer rain!

Chapter 7

Conclusions and Retrospect

In this short book I have tried to do two things: to provide a helpful overview of the current state of the academic study of the Psalms without ignoring the work of past scholars; and to offer my own, perhaps somewhat idiosyncratic, take on the subject. I hope that, without too much prejudice, I have made available a range of interpretations and approaches, while at the same time leaving no doubt as to my own position. The element of subjectivity and personal ownership which is implied by these two opening sentences is, I believe, essential to any honest contemporary presentation of topics within biblical studies. This is not to say that I think that everything is equally possible, or that I do not have strongly held opinions. Far from it – I am as convinced as I can be, without finally irrefutable proof, that David had nothing to do with writing any psalms, and I am equally convinced that the collection as we have it is largely and in essence a post-exilic production. But beyond these rather negative points, much remains unclear. What is clear is that thanks to an unprecedented expansion in the study of the Psalms, and aided by increasingly sophisticated analyses of the evidence from the Dead Sea, many fascinating theories have emerged in the last few decades. I hope that in the pages of this book some of that fascination (dare I suggest excitement, even?) has been communicated.

The arrangement of the book has been designed to open out a range of topics at the same time as covering a good proportion of the scholarly literature (principally in book or monograph form – it would be impossible in a work of this kind to review the journal material). The bibliography would in itself constitute an education in the subject; but since we are all busy people, I hope that readers of my book will be able to use it to guide them through the bibliographical maze to those resources which are of most relevance to them.

The Psalter has functioned throughout the centuries as a source of comfort, inspiration, liturgy, theology and poetry for two major religions and for those whose secularism is still identifiably Jewish or Christian. In my writing I have tried to acknowledge this fourfold audience (to which, perhaps, I should add a fifth: the disinterested scholar – though I have doubts about the existence of that fabulous species which, if it ever existed, is now seriously endangered). It may be that in attempting to cater for a wider readership I will only have succeeded in annoying everyone. On the other hand, it can be a useful learning process to encounter views which jolt us even a little out of our comfortable complacency. In any case, this book is only a starter. As I said in the first chapter, it is a kind of 'prequel' to my own *Psalms* (1999), and is something of a mixed genre. It is not strictly speaking an introduction, and it is not a commentary; it is neither a monograph nor an encyclopedia entry. I like to think of it as best described by an old-fashioned phrase: the *vade-mecum*. Literally meaning 'Go with me', a vade-mecum was, in the words of the *Shorter Oxford English Dictionary*, 'a book or manual suitable for carrying about with one for ready reference'. I'd be delighted to think that such might be the fate of this modest offering: better, at any rate, than lying dusty and unnoticed on a library shelf.

The only task left to me now is to say something about the range of introductions and commentaries on the Psalms. Many are rather old, and will perhaps only be found in well-stocked libraries; though there are increasing opportunities to find out-of-print items through the web. Both of the books by Cuthbert Keet which I have referred to in Chapters 2 and 5 are out of print, and I was only able to find them using http://www.abebooks.com/ which I can strongly recommend for this purpose. It does seem to me, however, important not to forget the past or let the work of scholars on whose endeavours we build be buried without trace, like the hidden strata in an archaeological site. There is, I believe, a duty of respect incumbent upon us, even if, practically speaking, we may have few reasons or opportunities to explore the work of our distant predecessors. That said, I shall end this short book with some descriptive notes on the extant range of introductions and commentaries.

1. Introductions to the Psalms

Gillingham (1994) and Seybold (1990) are perhaps the most convenient currently available introductions, in that they touch on most of the relevant topics, and are arranged in a reasonably friendly fashion.

John Day's contribution is shorter, and somewhat more restricted in that it focuses more on the forms of Psalms than do the other two; from this point of view it might usefully serve to complement what they offer. Christoph Barth's short study (1961 [1966]) is only about eighty pages in length, and inevitably shows its age. Nevertheless, Barth packs a lot into a short compass, and still has something to offer the enquiring mind. Westermann's *The Psalms: Structure, Content and Message* (1980) follows in the tradition of Gunkel, in a similar fashion to Day. It is because of Westermann's overall importance for the discipline that his introduction might still be of value. A similar tactic is to be found in Hayes's *Understanding the Psalms* (1976). A more expansive approach, covering both Wisdom and Poetry in the Old Testament, is taken by Donald K. Berry (1995). His book aims to give an overview of both subjects, and uses an overtly pedagogical technique. It has the advantage that it deals with the poetic traditions in the whole of the Old Testament and its cultural context. This necessitates a certain loss of depth, but that is made up for by the range of its interests.

More specialized volumes include Brenner and Fontaine (1998), on Wisdom and Psalms in the second series of the Feminist Companion to the Bible, Toni Craven (1992), who gives an introduction to spirituality and the Psalms, and Dennis Sylva (1993), whose *Psalms and the Transformation of Stress* offers a psychoanalytic interpretation of selected psalms. The subject of feminism and the Psalms is one that I have, admittedly, not reviewed in this book. My failure to do so is no indication that I do not take it seriously, and I recommend this collection as a way of beginning to fill that particular gap. Nor, as it happens, have I referred to post-colonial readings and the Psalms; here I am more at a loss, since I am not aware of any introductory work in this field of Psalms studies.

Several collections of essays deserve mention. Two volumes, representing somewhat different traditions, provide similar collections of essays on a range of relevant topics. Clines (1997) reprints a selection of articles first published in JSOT, including two key contributions by Walter Brueggeman and Gerald Wilson; the collection edited by Johnston and Firth (2005) covers an interesting range of themes and issues from a broadly evangelical perspective. Flint and Miller (2005) is a more daunting prospect. For a start it is really only accessible (because of its price) as a library resource, and its purpose is to provide a rather high-level overview of Psalms scholarship. Taken together, these three collections represent a solid source of advanced work on the Psalms for those who wish to go beyond the present vade-mecum.

My own contribution (1999) sits somewhere in the middle. It is not an introduction, rather it sets out to provide a new kind of structured approach to the work of Psalms commentary and interpretation. Thus is serves both as a study of methodology and as a series of 'worked examples' (specifically Psalms 2; 8; 24; 29; 74; 82; and the Psalms of Ascents: 120–34). It concludes with a detailed proposal about a contextual interpretation of how the Psalms of Ascents may have functioned in the last two centuries BCE.

2. Commentaries

For the most part commentaries serve as a source of introductory material, as a catalogue of scholarly work in the field up to the date of publication, and as a way into the specific detail of individual passages, whether one's quest is to do with puzzles in the text, queries about its context, interest in its intertextuality, or a desire to explore its afterlife in the hands of interpreters. Some commentaries are deliberately aimed at a professional readership (P), others at a lay or church or synagogue audience (L). Some aspire to be as scientifically objective as the discipline allows (O), others are expressly directed to the kind of interpretation that will be acceptable to a religiously committed readership (C). In itemizing the following list of commentaries I have tried to provide information relating to these various authorial intentions; such information is, of course, very rough and ready, and should not be taken as a definitive taxonomy. In addition I have taken a somewhat arbitrary cut-off point in 1960 to distinguish 'modern' from 'pre-modern' commentaries. These in turn do not go further back than the nineteenth century; a list of what might be described as 'classical' commentaries is to be found at the end of Chapter 3.

One study in particular should be mentioned here. Eaton's *Psalms of the Way and the Kingdom: A Conference with the Commentators* (1995) examines three 'torah' psalms (1; 19; 119) and three royal psalms (93; 97; 99) by means of a metaphorical discussion with a wide range of commentators from Delitzsch to Dahood. His explicit decision to engage directly with the commentary tradition means that this book affords a way in for those who would like to get a flavour of their work without having to read the commentaries themselves.

a. Modern commentaries (post-1960)

The list of commentaries published in the last forty years or so is daunting. The majority are what might best be described as technical; that is, they should be categorized as (P) in the taxonomy above; the others are designated as (L). Within these overall categories, some come from an openly evangelical publishing house: these I have indicated as (O, C); the others I have marked as simply (O). This admittedly crude diagnosis takes no account of where individual scholars may hang their hat; in any case, all of these commentaries will serve the primary purposes indicated at the beginning of this section.

Professional commentaries (P)

(O, C)   Kidner (1973, 1975); Allen (1983); Craigie (1983); Tate (1990); Goldingay (2006)
(O)   Weiser (1962); Dahood (1970); Anderson (1972); Kraus (1988, 1989); Clifford (2002, 2003); Terrien (2003); Hossfeld and Zenger (2005)

The commentaries in these two groups vary considerably in detail. Allen, Craigie and Tate from the first group, and Kraus and Hossfeld and Zenger from the second provide very extensive technical detail. Dahood has a very special interest: to demonstrate a maximum degree of dependence of Israel's Psalms on the language and liturgical myths of Ugarit; and Terrien has a special concern for the strophic patterns of each individual psalm.

Lay commentaries (L)

Mowvley (1989); Davidson (1998); Eaton (2003); Curtis (2004)

There is of course a much greater range of commentaries in this section than I have noted here. The four listed are all by established scholars who have chosen to relate their work to the specific needs of the community of faith; indeed the full title of Robert Davidson's *The Vitality of Worship* makes that explicitly clear. Mowvley describes his book as *The Psalms: Introduced and Newly Translated for Today's Readers*, another self-explanatory title, while Eaton includes the phrase 'a historical and spiritual commentary'. The important point in all of these examples is that scholars of repute, with a solid basis in the critical study of the Old Testament, have chosen this means to communicate beyond the cloisters, in an attempt to bridge the chasm that all too often gapes between the world of the academy on the one hand, and the ongoing life of the church and synagogue on the other. In regard to the latter, the books noted in Chapter 6 by Magonet and Sarna serve a similar purpose.

b. Pre-modern commentaries (before 1960)

(O)   Ewald (1880–81); Delitzsch (1887–89); Briggs (1907, 1909). Ewald and Delitzsch are representative of the new German biblical scholarship which led the field in the nineteenth century; the Briggses (husband and wife – a rare team in our field) wrote the Psalms volume in the International Critical Commentary, whose avowed aim was to make the finest critical scholarship widely available to the English-speaking world.

(O, C) Maclaren (1893). This is the Psalms volume in the Expositor's Bible, whose title speaks for itself. A modern equivalent is the Interpreter's Bible.

(O, L) Kirkpatrick (1902). This is the Psalms volume in the first Cambridge Commentary series – designed for the intelligent lay reader.

And with these few recommendations I conclude, in the hope that I have not contributed yet another proof of Qoheleth's bleak dictum (Eccl. 12.12):

> Of making many books there is no end,
> and much study is a weariness of the flesh.

Bibliography

The Bibliography lists all the works cited in the body of the text except the two special lists at the end of Chapters 2 and 3.

Abegg, Martin, Jr, Peter Flint and Eugene Ulrich (eds).
    1999   *The Dead Sea Scrolls Bible* (New York: HarperCollins).
Allen, L.C.
    1983   *Psalms 101–150* (Word Biblical Commentary 21; Waco: Word Books).
Alter, R.
    1980   *The Art of Biblical Poetry* (Edinburgh: T & T Clark).
Anderson, A.A.
    1972   *Psalms 1–72; Psalms 73–150* (2 vols; New Century Bible; London: Marshall, Morgan & Scott).
Anderson, B.W.
    1983   *Out of the Depths: The Psalms Speak for Us Today* (Philadelphia: Westminster John Knox Press; London: SCM Press).
Attridge, Harold W. and Margot E. Fassler (eds).
    2003   *Psalms in Community: Jewish and Christian Textual, Liturgical, and Artistic Traditions* (Leiden: Brill).
Barth, C.F.
    1961 [1966] *Introduction to the Psalms* (Oxford: Blackwell).
Barton, John.
    1996   *Reading the Old Testament: Method in Biblical Study* (London: Darton, Longman & Todd, 2nd edn).
Bekkenkamp, Jonneke and Yvonne Sherwood (eds).
    2003   *Sanctified Aggression: Legacies of Biblical and Post-Biblical Vocabularies of Violence* (Bible in the Twenty-first Century Series 3; JSOT Supp. 400; London: T& T Clark).
Berlin, A.
    1985   *The Dynamics of Biblical Parallelism* (Bloomington: Indiana University Press).
Berry, Donald K.
    1995   *An Introduction to Wisdom and Poetry of the Old Testament* (Nashville: Broadman & Holman).

Beyerlin, W. (ed.).
 1978   *Near Eastern Texts Relating to the Old Testament* (Old Testament
               Library; London: SCM Press).
Brenner, A. and C. Fontaine (eds).
 1998   *Wisdom and Psalms* (The Feminist Companion to the Bible,
               Second Series, 2; Sheffield: Sheffield Academic Press).
Briggs, C.A. and E.G.
 1907, 1909   *The Psalms* (ICC Commentary; 2 vols; Edinburgh: T & T
               Clark).
Brown, William P.
 2002   *Seeing the Psalms: A Theology of Metaphor* (Louisville and
               London: Westminster John Knox Press).
Broyles, C.C.
 1989   *The Conflict of Faith and Experience in the Psalms* (Sheffield:
               JSOT Press).
Brueggemann, W.
 1980   'Psalms and the Life of Faith: A Suggested Typology of Function',
               JSOT 17 (1980), pp. 3–32.
 1984   *The Message of the Psalms* (London: SCM Press).
 1990   'Bounded by Obedience and Praise: The Psalms as Canon', *JSOT*
               50 (1990), pp. 63–92.
 1991   *Abiding Astonishment: Psalms, Modernity and the Making of
               History* (Philadelphia: Westminster John Knox Press; London:
               SCM Press).
Carmi, T.
 1981   *The Penguin Book of Hebrew Verse* (Harmondsworth: Penguin
               Books).
Carroll, Robert P.
 1981   *From Chaos to Covenant: Uses of Prophecy in the Book of
               Jeremiah* (London: SCM Press).
Childs B.S.
 1979   *Introduction to the Old Testament as Scripture* (London: SCM
               Press).
Clifford, Richard J.
 2002   *Psalms 1–72* (Abingdon Old Testament Commentaries; Nashville:
               Abingdon Press).
 2003   *Psalms 73–150* (Abingdon Old Testament Commentaries;
               Nashville: Abingdon Press).
Clines, David A. J. (ed.).
 1997   *The Poetical Books* (Sheffield: Sheffield Academic Press).
Cole, Robert L.
 2000   *The Shape and Message of Book III* (Sheffield: Sheffield Academic
               Press).

Craigie, P.C.
  1983   *Psalms 1–50* (Waco: Word Books).
Craven, T.
  1992   *The Book of Psalms* (Message of Biblical Spirituality 6;
            Collegeville: Liturgical Press).
Creach, Jerome F.D.
  1996   *The Choice of Yahweh as Refuge and the Editing of the Hebrew
            Psalter* (Sheffield: Sheffield Academic Press).
Crow, Loren D.
  1996   *The Songs of Ascents (Psalms 120–134): Their Place in Israelite
            History and Religion* (Atlanta: Scholars Press).
Culley, R.C.
  1967   *Oral Formulaic Language in the Biblical Psalms* (Toronto:
            University of Toronto Press).
Curtis, Adrian.
  2004   *Psalms* (Epworth Commentaries; Peterborough: Epworth Press).
Dahood, M.
  1970   *Psalms* (Anchor Bible; 3 vols; New York: Doubleday).
Danby, H.
  1933   *The Mishnah: Translated from the Hebrew with Introduction and
            Brief Explanatory Notes* (Oxford: Clarendon Press).
Davidson, R.
  1998   *The Vitality of Worship* (Edinburgh: Handsel Press).
Davie, Donald (ed.).
  1996   *The Psalms in English* (Harmondsworth: Penguin Classics).
Day, J.
  1990   *Psalms* (Old Testament Guides; Sheffield: JSOT Press).
deClaissé-Walford, Nancy.
  1997   *Reading from the Beginning: The Shaping of the Hebrew Psalter*
            (Macon, GA: Mercer University Press).
Delitzsch, F.
  1887–89   *The Psalms* (3 vols; London: Hodder & Stoughton).
Eaton, John H.
  1986   *Kingship and the Psalms* (Sheffield: JSOT Press, 2nd edn).
  1995   *Psalms of the Way and the Kingdom: A Conference with the
            Commentators* (Sheffield: Sheffield Academic Press).
  2003   *The Psalms: A Historical and Spiritual Commentary with
            an Introduction and New Translation* (London: T & T Clark
            International).
Ewald, G.H.A.
  1880–81   *Commentary on the Psalms* (London: Williams & Norgate).
Finkelstein, Israel and Neil Asher Silberman.
  2002   *The Bible Unearthed: Archaeology's New Vision of Ancient*

Israel and the Origin of its Sacred Texts (New York: Simon & Schuster).

Fisch, H.

1988   *Poetry with a Purpose: Biblical Poetics and Interpretation* (Bloomington: Indiana University Press).

Flint, P.W.

1997   *The Dead Sea Psalms Scrolls and the Book of Psalms* (STDJ 17; Leiden and New York: Brill).

Flint, P.W. and P.D. Miller (eds).

2005   *The Book of Psalms: Composition and Reception* (Leiden: Brill).

Fokkelman, J.P.

2001   *Reading Biblical Poetry: An Introductory Guide* (Louisville and London: Westminster John Knox Press).

2002   *The Psalms in Form: The Hebrew Psalter in its Poetic Shape* (Leiden: Deo).

Freer, Coburn.

1972   *Music for a King: George Herbert's Style and the Metrical Psalms* (Baltimore and London: Johns Hopkins University Press).

Frost, David L., J.A. Emerton and A.A. Macintosh.

1977   *The Psalms: A New Translation for Worship* (London: Collins).

Gelineau, Joseph.

1963   *The Psalms: A New Translation. Translated from the Hebrew and Arranged for Singing to the Psalmody of Joseph Gelineau* (Fontana Books; London & Glasgow: Collins).

Gerstenberger, E.S.

1988   *Psalms: With an Introduction to Cultic Poetry. Part 1* (Forms of OT Literature, 14; Grand Rapids: Eerdmans).

2001   *Psalms. Part 2, and Lamentations* (Forms of OT Literature, 15; Grand Rapids: Eerdmans).

Gillingham, S.E.

1994   *The Poems and Psalms of the Hebrew Bible* (Oxford: Oxford University Press).

Goldingay, John.

2006   *Psalms* (Grand Rapids: Baker Academic).

Goulder, M.D.

1982   *The Psalms of the Sons of Korah* (Sheffield: JSOT Press).

1990   *The Prayers of David (Psalms 51–72)* (Sheffield: Sheffield Academic Press).

1996   *The Psalms of Asaph and the Pentateuch* (Studies in the Psalter III; Sheffield: Sheffield Academic Press).

1998   *The Psalms of the Return* (Sheffield: Sheffield Academic Press).

Gunkel, Hermann.

1933 [1998] *Introduction to the Psalms* (completed by Joachim Begrich; trans.

James D. Nogalski; Macon, GA: Mercer University Press).

Harris, Robert A.
2004   *Discerning Parallelism: A Study in Northern French Medieval Jewish Biblical Exegesis* (Brown Judaic Studies 341; Providence, RI: Brown University).

Hayes, J.H.
1976   *Understanding the Psalms* (Valley Forge: Judson Press).

Holladay, W.L.
1993   *The Psalms Through Three Thousand Years* (Minneapolis: Fortress Press).

Hossfeld, F.L and E. Zenger.
2005   *Psalms 2* (Hermeneia; Minneapolis: Fortress Press).

Howard, David M.
1997   *The Structure of Psalms 93–100* (Winona Lake: Eisenbrauns).

Hunter, A.G.
1999   *Psalms* (Old Testament Readings; London: Routledge).
2004   'The Missing/Mystical Messiah: Melchizedek Among the Specters of Genesis 14,' in Y. Sherwood (ed.), *Derrida's Bible* (New York: Palgrave), 81–97.

Jackson, Gordon.
1997   *The Lincoln Psalter* (Manchester: Carcanet).

Jacobson, David C.
1996   *Does David Still Play Before You?* (Detroit: Wayne State University Press).

Johnson, A.R.
1955 [1962] *Sacral Kingship in Ancient Israel* (Cardiff: University of Wales Press, 2nd edn).

Johnston, Phillip S. and David G. Firth.
2005   *Interpreting the Psalms: Issues and Approaches* (Leicester: Apollos)

Kartun-Blum, Ruth.
1999   *Profane Scriptures* (Cincinnati: Hebrew Union College Press).

Katz, Steven T.
1983   *Post-Holocaust Dialogues: Critical Studies in Modern Jewish Thought* (New York: New York University Press).

Keel, Othmar.
1978   *The Symbolism of the Biblical World: Ancient Near Eastern Iconography and the Book of Psalms* (London: SPCK).

Keet, C.C.
1928   *A Liturgical Study of the Psalter* (London: George Allen & Unwin).
1969   *A Study of the Psalms of Ascent* (London: Mitre Press).

Kidner, D.
  1973   *Psalms 1–72*. (Tyndale Old Testament Commentary; London:
            Inter-Varsity Press).
  1975   *Psalms 73–150* (Tyndale Old Testament Commentary; London:
            Inter-Varsity Press).
Kirkpatrick, A.F.
  1902   *The Psalms* (Cambridge Bible for Schools and Colleges; Cambridge:
            Cambridge University Press).
Kraus, H.-J.
  1988   *Psalms 1–59* (Minneapolis: Fortress Press).
  1989   *Psalms 60–150* (Minneapolis: Fortress Press).
  1992   *Theology of the Psalms* (Minneapolis: Fortress Press).
Kugel, J.L.
  1981   *The Idea of Biblical Poetry: Parallelism and its History* (New
            Haven and London: Yale University Press).
Levi, Peter.
  1976   *The Psalms* (Penguin Classics; Harmondsworth: Penguin Books).
Levine, Herbert J.
  1995   *Sing Unto God a New Song* (Bloomington: Indiana University
            Press).
Lewis, C.S.
  1958   *Reflections on the Psalms* (London: Geoffrey Bles).
Lord, Albert B.
  1960   *The Singer of Tales* (Cambridge, MA: Harvard University
            Press).
Lowth, Robert.
  1787 [1847] *Lectures on the Sacred Poetry of the Hebrews* (trans. G. Gregory;
            London: S. Chadwick & Co.).
Mackenzie, Norman H. (ed.).
  1990   *The Poetical Works of Gerard Manley Hopkins* (Oxford:
            Clarendon Press).
Maclaren, A.
  1893   *The Psalms* (Expositor's Bible; London: Hodder & Stoughton).
Magonet, J.
  1994   *A Rabbi Reads the Psalms* (London: SCM).
Manser, Martin H. (ed.).
  2003   *The Bible: New Revised Standard Version* (Cross-Reference
            Edition, consultant editors John Barton and Bruce M. Metzger;
            Oxford: Oxford University Press).
Mays, J.L.
  1994   *The Lord Reigns: A Theological Handbook to the Psalms*
            (Louisville: Westminster John Knox Press).

Mazor, Yair.
  2003   *The Poetry of Asher Reich: Portrait of a Hebrew Poet* (Madison: University of Wisconsin Press).

McCann, J.C. (ed.).
  1993a   *The Shape and Shaping of the Psalter* (Sheffield: Sheffield Academic Press).
  1993b   *A Theological Introduction to the Book of Psalms: The Psalms as Torah* (Nashville: Abingdon Press)

McKnight, Edgar V.
  1985   *The Bible and the Reader: An Introduction to Literary Criticism* (Philadelphia: Fortress Press).

Mowinckel, S.
  1962   *The Psalms in Israel's Worship* (2 vols; Oxford: Blackwell).

Mowvley, Harry.
  1989   *The Psalms: Introduced and Newly Translated for Today's Readers* (London: Collins).

Moyise, Steve and Maarten J.J. Menken.
  2004   *The Psalms in the New Testament* (The New Testament and the Scriptures of Israel; London and New York: T & T Clark).

Nasuti, H.P.
  1988   *Tradition History and the Psalms of Asaph* (Atlanta: Scholars Press).
  1998   *Defining the Sacred Songs: Genre, Tradition and Post-critical Interpretation of the Psalms* (Sheffield: Sheffield Academic Press).

Neusner, Jacob, W.S. Green and E. Frerichs (eds).
  1987   *Judaisms and Their Messiahs at the Turn of the Christian Era* (Cambridge: Cambridge University Press).

Patrides, C.A. (ed.).
  1974   *The English Poems of George Herbert* (Everyman's University Library; London: J.M. Dent & Sons).

Perrin, Norman.
  1970   *What is Redaction Criticism?* (London: SPCK).

Petersen, David L. and K.H. Richards (eds).
  1992   *Interpreting Hebrew Poetry* (Minneapolis: Fortress Press).

Pritchard, R.E. (ed.).
  1992   *The Sidney Psalms* (Fyfield Books; Manchester: Carcanet Press).

Prothero, Rowland E.
  1914   *The Psalms in Human Life* (London: John Murray, 4th edn).

Radzinowicz, Mary Ann.
  1989   *Milton's Epics and the Book of Psalms* (Princeton: Princeton University Press).

Ryrie, Alexander.
   2004   *Deliver Us from Evil: Reading the Psalms as Poetry* (London: Darton, Longman & Todd).

Sanders, J.A.
   1967   *The Dead Sea Psalms Scroll* (Ithaca, NY: Cornell University Press).

Sarna, Nahum.
   1993   *On the Book of Psalms* (New York: Schocken).

Seybold, K.
   1990   *Introducing the Psalms* (Edinburgh: T & T Clark).

Shires, Henry M.
   1974   *Finding the Old Testament in the New* (Philadelphia: Westminster Press).

Slavitt, David R.
   1996   *Sixty-One Psalms of David* (New York and Oxford: Oxford University Press).

Smith, A.J.
   1976   *John Donne: The Complete English Poems* (Harmondsworth: Penguin Books).

Starbuck, Scott A.
   1999   *Court Oracles in the Psalms* (Atlanta: Scholars Press).

Sylva, Dennis.
   1993   *Psalms and the Transformation of Stress* (Grand Rapids: Eerdmans).

Tate, M.E.
   1990   *Psalms 51–100* (Waco: Word Books).

Terrien, Samuel L.
   2003   *The Psalms: Strophic Structure and Theological Commentary* (Grand Rapids and Cambridge: Eerdmans).

Tomes, Roger.
   2005   *I Have Written to the King, My Lord: Secular Analogies for the Psalms* (Hebrew Bible Monographs, 1; Sheffield: Phoenix Press).

Trible, Phyllis.
   1978   *God and the Rhetoric of Sexuality* (Philadelphia: Fortress Press).

Trudinger, Peter L.
   2004   *The Psalms of the Tamid Service* (Leiden: Brill).

Tubb, Jonathan.
   2006   *Canaanites* (Peoples of the Past; London: British Museum Press, rev. edn).

van Rooy, Harry F.
   2005   'The Psalms in Early Syriac Tradition', in P.W. and P.D. Miller (eds), *The Book of Psalms: Composition and Reception* (Leiden:

Brill), pp. 537–50.

Vermes, Geza.

1997   *The Complete Dead Sea Scrolls in English* (Harmondsworth: Penguin Press).

Wallace, Howard N.

2005   *Words to God, Word from God: The Psalms in the Prayer and Preaching of the Church* (Aldershot: Ashgate).

Watson, W.G.E.

1984   *Classical Hebrew Poetry* (Sheffield: JSOT Press).

Watters, William.

1976   *Formula Criticism and the Poetry of the Old Testament* (BZAW 138; New York: Walter De Gruyter).

Watts, J.W.

1992   *Psalm and Story: Inset Hymns in Hebrew Narrative* (Sheffield: Sheffield Academic Press).

Weiser, A.

1962   *The Psalms* (The Old Testament Library; London: SCM Press).

Westermann, C.

1980   *The Psalms: Structure, Content and Message* (Minneapolis: Augsburg).

1981   *Praise and Lament in the Psalms* (Edinburgh: T & T Clark).

Wieder, Laurance (ed.).

1995   *The Poets' Book of Psalms* (New York and Oxford: Oxford University Press).

2003   *Words to God's Music: A New Book of Psalms* (Grand Rapids: Eerdmans).

Wilson, G.H.

1985   *The Editing of the Hebrew Psalter* (Chico: Scholars Press).

Wilson, R.R.

1980   *Prophecy and Society in Ancient Israel* (Philadelphia: Fortress Press).

Index of Topics

Note: References to specific psalms have not been indexed. Other Biblical books have been indexed where there is a substantial reference to them in relation to Psalms

Index of Modern Authors